Bridget Bryant graduated in sociology at the London School of Economics and subsequently worked in the MRC Social Psychiatry Research Unit at the Maudsley Hospital, in the Bedford College Social Research Unit, and at the Department of Experimental Psychology, University of Oxford. Her main interests have been in social psychiatry and child welfare, and she is co-author of two books and five papers. She is now working in the Department of Psychiatry at the University of Oxford, and is married with three children.

Miriam Harris graduated in psychology at the University of Liverpool, and then worked as a research assistant at the Tavistock Institute of Human Relations. After varied fieldwork on a wide range of projects she spent six years on research administration at the Social Science Research Council, mainly with the Psychology Committee. When the Oxford Preschool Research Group was set up, she was seconded by the SSRC as administrator and research coordinator, and combined that role with research into the subject of this book. She now works for the Nuffield Foundation.

Dee Newton graduated in sociology at the University of Leicester, and was a child care officer for the London Borough of Islington. After qualifying in social work at the University of Birmingham she became a community worker and later undertook research into administrative tribunals. She has helped set up new preschool provision in both Birmingham and Oxford, and researched part-time in the preschool field, for the Department of Social and Administrative Studies, University of Oxford. She is married with two children.

The Oxford Preschool Research Project

Children and Minders

Bridget Bryant, Miriam Harris
and Dee Newton

THE
HIGH/SCOPE
PRESS

First published in England (1980) by
Grant McIntyre Ltd
39 Great Russell Street
London WC1B 3PH

**THE
HIGH/SCOPE
   PRESS**
a division of
High/Scope Educational Research Foundation
600 North River Street
Ypsilanti, MI 48197
(313) 485-2000

Library of Congress Cataloging in
Publication Data.

Bryant, Bridget.
  Children and minders.
  (Oxford preschool research project;
3) Bibliography: p. Includes index.
  1. Day care centers—Great Britain.
  I. Harris, Miriam, joint author.
  II. Newton, Dee, joint author. III. Title.
  IV. Series.
  HV861.G6B78   1980
  362.7'12'0941   80-24692
  ISBN 0-931114-11-X (pbk.)

Contents

For Peter, John and Ken
and especially
for Daniel, Naomi, Emma, Rebecca and Camilla
who had to share their mothers with the minded children
while this book was being written

*'How many times must the clock go round before Mummy
comes?'*

A MINDED CHILD

Foreword by Jack Wrigley

In 1971, when a massive expansion of nursery education in Britain was proposed, there was relatively little easily available evidence to suggest how best this should be done. Consequently the Department of Education and Science and the Scottish Education Department initiated a programme of research on nursery education to answer practical questions about provision and to study the effects of expansion. The Educational Research Board of the Social Science Research Council saw the need for a complementary research programme concerned as well with some more fundamental issues which covered the whole range of preschool education.

The work was coordinated in the Department of Education and Science by a management committee on which the Schools Council and SSRC were represented. The original idea, that SSRC should concentrate on fundamental research while DES funded more policy oriented and practical work, proved too simple. What quickly emerged was a view that much of the fundamental work on preschool children had already been carried out. What was lacking was the dissemination of that knowledge and its implementation in the field. Within SSRC a preschool working group was given the task of commissioning projects, and the work of the Oxford Preschool Research Group, under Professor Bruner, reported in this series of publications, was the main element in the first phase of the SSRC programme.

Professor Bruner had already accomplished distinguished fundamental work in this field and was therefore well placed to make the point of the need for dissemination and implementation. Despite the many changes in the economic and political scene in the 1970s the original gap in knowledge remains important and the results of the SSRC research programme will do much to fill the gap. In particular, Professor Bruner's work in Oxfordshire has great value for the rest of the country. The publications of the Oxford Preschool Research Group, together with the results from other participants in the programme, will help give a firmer base on which to build for the future.

Jack Wrigley
Chairman
SSRC Educational Research
Board Panel on
Accountability in
London, 1979   Education

Foreword by Jerome Bruner

This book is one in a series that emerges from the Oxford Preschool Research Group. Like the others in the series, it is concerned with the provision of care in Britain for the preschool child away from home and is the result of several years of research devoted to various aspects of that issue. There are few more controversial and crucial issues facing Britain today. The objective of the series is to shed light on present needs, on the quality of care available and on the extent to which this care meets these needs. The general aim is to provide a basis for discussion of future policy.

The studies have all been financed by the Social Science Research Council of Great Britain. They were commissioned in 1974, a year or two after Mrs Thatcher's White Paper, *Education: a Framework for Expansion,* was published, at a time when it was thought that there would be a publicly financed expansion of preschool care and education in Britain. Since that time events have caught up with the enterprise and Britain finds itself in a period of economic stringency during which many of the hoped-for changes will have to be shelved until better days come again. Nonetheless, the studies are opportune, for careful study and planning will be necessary not only to meet present needs with reduced resources, but to shape policy and practice for an improved future service on behalf of children in Britain and their families.

Developmental studies of the past two decades have pointed increasingly to the importance of the opening years of life for the intellectual, social, and emotional growth of human beings. The books in this series, it is hoped, shed light on the practical steps that must be taken to assure that the early years can contribute to the well-being of a next generation in Britain.

Oxford, 1979   *Jerome Bruner*

Acknowledgements

The research on which this book is based could not have been done without the help and support of many people, and we welcome this opportunity to thank them all.

We should like to express our warm appreciation of the many colleagues and friends who contributed their talents to our work in various ways and at different times. We are especially indebted to Sue North, who carried out most of the interviews and contributed greatly to their success. We would also like to thank Jerry Bruner and all our colleagues in the Oxford Preschool Research Group for their helpful criticisms and suggestions over the three years of the project. We would also like to thank members of the Thomas Coram Research Unit, particularly Berry Mayall and Pat Petrie, whose work on minded children contributed greatly to our own, and Jack and Barbara Tizard. Jack Tizard was one of the first people to become concerned about minded children, and in his recent sad death children everywhere have lost one of their most compassionate and eloquent champions.

We are grateful to the Social Science Research Council for their generous financial support; to the Oxfordshire Social Services Department, especially David Hawley, R. A. Wood, Helen Brooks and Julia Dray, whose cooperation made our task much easier; and to Paul Griffiths of the Oxford University Computer Centre.

We should also like to thank Joanna Boyce and Sasha Metaxas, who typed questionnaires and drafts and in general kept us organized; and Jacqueline Selby, who helped to type the final version.

Finally, we are deeply grateful to the minders and mothers for their generosity and good nature in allowing us into their homes and giving us so much of their time. By the same token we must also thank the children (too young to agree or disagree) who had to do without attention for what must have seemed a very long time—and especially the children who saw their mothers very little during the week and whose precious weekends we invaded.

1
What do we know about minding?

> The present childminding system is so seriously deficient that only root and branch reform can hope to achieve standards which are satisfactory.

> A particularly positive aspect of day care in a family is the opportunity it provides for the child to make the close, personal, continuing relationships that are so essential as the foundation of sound emotional development.

The first of these quotations is taken from a report on facilities for working mothers prepared by the Trades Union Congress; the second from a speech at a conference made by a senior civil servant at the Department of Health and Social Security. They already give us an idea of the controversy surrounding minding as a form of day care for young children. Much of this controversy is based on myths and assumptions about the quality of this care rather than a knowledge of what actually happens to minded children, and it will be the task of this book to try to unravel some of these myths. First, though, we must set the scene.

What is a childminder? She is a woman* who looks after other people's children between the ages of zero and five years, for at least two hours a day, and for reward. By law she must be registered with her local authority if she is not a close relative of the child. Since 1971 responsibility for childminders has lain with the social services departments, who took over from the health departments.

---

* We have heard of one male registered childminder, and there may be others, but for convenience we will use the female designation throughout this book.

How has minding come about and how many children are involved? Minding goes back a long way, to the Industrial Revolution and the first employment of women outside their homes in factories, mills and mines. Its early history and growth is excellently described by Tizard, Moss and Perry (1976) in *All our Children*. They also describe the dramatic trend all over Europe in recent years for mothers of young children to go out to work in ever greater numbers. Even in the last decade the proportion of working mothers with children under five has risen from 19 per cent in 1971 (*1971 Census*) to 26 per cent in 1974 (Bone, 1977).

Some have suggested that recent economic difficulties in Britain may have lessened the demand for day care, but there is no evidence to support this. Others have argued that recession and inflation have had the opposite effect, and that the erosion in value of husbands' incomes is sending more wives out to work to maintain their families' living standards. The London Council of Social Service, in its report in 1977, took the view that 'it may well be that more women are seeking work, in which case the need for child minders will increase even further' (LCSS 1977). Margaret Bone, studying the need for day care, found in addition to the quarter of mothers of preschool·children already working a further fifth who said they would like to work if they could find satisfactory care for their children.

How many children are minded? There is considerable confusion over this. According to a study by the Local Authorities Association there were up to 65,000 children being cared for full time by registered minders in 1976.* In addition there is the unknown number looked after by illegal minders, which has, as we shall see, been variously estimated as enormous and as not very great. Whatever the exact figure, it is clear that many thousands of children are minded, and even if they represent only a tiny proportion of all young children, they are, as has so often been said, in the

---

* These figures cover places for which minders are registered, and not minded children. They were collected in a rather ambiguous way, and it is not clear whether they sometimes include home playgroups.

most formative and defenceless period of their lives, and as a society as well as parents we have a responsibility towards them and what becomes of them.

What is happening to minding now? In recent years it has become the subject of a good deal of debate, interest and action. There are moves afoot to get the law governing registration changed; minders themselves are starting to become organized; social workers are trying to provide 'support' services and training courses in many parts of the country; others in government circles are pointing to the advantages of minding over other forms of day care, namely that it costs the government little, and that it is in theory the nearest substitute to 'being at home with mum'. Even if the government does nothing to intervene, which seems the likeliest course of events for a good few years, minding will continue to expand as a form of provision, filling the gap left by the failure of day nurseries and nursery schools, of which there are totally inadequate numbers, to meet need and demand.

This gap itself seems likely to widen. Not only has the expansion of nursery schools come to a halt, but there have even been cuts in nursery provision in some areas. Not that nursery schools are a great deal of help for working mothers, since their hours are too limited: but if one looks at public provision of day nurseries, where the hours are more suited to the needs of the working mother, one finds it so scarce in most areas as to be unobtainable except for a small number of 'priority' children. Given the need or opportunity to work, many more mothers will have no option but to use minders. At the same time renewed and serious doubt is being cast on minding from other quarters, which argue not for expansion of the existing system but for a completely new approach. All these different moves and opinions were already evident when we started our study in 1976, and have intensified considerably since.

This is by way of a very brief introduction to minding. In the rest of this chapter we shall look in greater detail at the professional debate over the past ten years, at the view parents have taken, and lastly at the way childminders themselves have viewed themselves and their work. We hope this will begin to clarify what is established fact and what is myth and rhetoric.

The professional debate

Focus on bad practice

In the late sixties and early seventies a few professionals interested in childminding concentrated on scandal and bad practice, and used the mass media to make their views known. Most prominent were Brian and Sonia Jackson, who tried to draw attention to what they saw as an intolerable state of affairs; they described it as one in which thousands of children, particularly in the inner areas of large cities, were spending each day in inadequate, overcrowded and unstimulating conditions, badly cared for physically and suffering from frequent moves from one minder to another. They gave graphic examples and made dramatic estimates of the number of illegal minders, which they claimed probably exceeded those registered in the ratio of ten to one in some areas. The following quotations (Jackson, 1973) are typical of the statements being made during this period.

> In Birmingham I met Mrs Griffiths. She kept six toddlers (four black and two white) on an old white linen sheet in her sort-of-front-hall for twelve hours a day. They did nothing: really nothing.

> My most unacceptable experience was finding rows of pink and royal blue carrycots (in each a small baby) parked like packaged battery chickens in a garage; and for this the mothers paid £3.00 per week.

By the mid-seventies, many social workers had become worried in the same way, judging by the enormous burgeoning of activity on the part of both voluntary bodies like the Elfrida Rathbone Society and local authority social services departments, particularly in London. There were the Bunbury projects in Islington and Lewisham (Shinman, 1979), the Angell Day Care Project, the Groveway project in Lambeth (Willmott and Challis, 1977), the Van Leer Project in Birmingham, to name just a few examples of attempts made in different ways to improve the quality of minding.

Some local authorities made small scale studies of minding in their areas around this time (for example, Cornwall Social Services Department) and various groups studied the demand for day care in general, including minding, in their areas (for example the Harrow branch of the National Campaign for Nursery Education together with the Harrow Social Services Department).

All this concern, and the action based on it, was tied in with the issue of registration. It is worth digressing briefly here to consider exactly what registration involves. The basic framework is laid down in the Nurseries and Childminders Regulation Act of 1948. Under this Act, and the amendments to it in the Health Services and Public Health Act 1968, and the Local Authority Social Services Act 1970, anyone looking after a child who is not a relative for more than two hours a day in her own home for reward must be registered by the Local Social Services Department; each Department has to keep a register of all such persons, and has the power to regulate minding in its own area. The sections of the act dealing with criteria for registration, other than stipulating that a minder shall be '*a fit person for looking after children*' (defined by the 1948 Act in terms of not having been previously disqualified from working with children by committing offences under the Children Act and Adoption Act), concentrate on physical conditions – housing, safety, heating, ventilation, protection against infectious diseases, record keeping, and so forth. These criteria are very unspecific and leave much to local authorities' interpretation, although guidelines (for instance on desirable numbers) are contained in DHSS circulars, which have been issued from time to time.* The Acts also lay down penalties for not registering or for breaching the conditions of registration and set up an appeals procedure for cases where an application for registration is refused. Between 1972 and 1976 there were three prosecutions for failure to register; one resulted in a fine, and the outcome of the other two is not known. No figures are available for prosecutions for breaching conditions of registration, nor for appeals against refusal to register.

This very minimal procedure, then, is the context in which discussion and debate took off in the late 1960s and early 1970s. A belief had grown up then, based particularly on Brian Jackson's claims, that enormous numbers of illegal minders co-existed beside the registered ones, and that these on the whole were the women providing the grossly unsatisfactory care. Nobody has ever proved either that these vast numbers exist or that they provide worse care than registered minders. Where researchers have tried very hard to locate unregistered minders they have rarely found very many. For example, Barbara Osborne (1975) describes how she interviewed groups of mothers of under-fives, some of whom were working and some not, and asked them questions about who cared for their children and whether they themselves were minders. This exercise produced the names and addresses of 30 registered minders but only three unregistered. She did add that she might have got another six of each if the mothers had been willing to pass on their addresses, but this would only have brought the total to 36 registered and nine unregistered. Moreover she found that 'the mothers were just as likely to be dissatisfied with their registered as with their unregistered minders.' This finding, however, conflicts with that of the Community Relations Commission in their report *Who Minds?* (CRC, 1975) that 'Childminders, when registered, [are] a popular form of child care with mothers and most dissatisfaction is felt with unregistered minders.'

* For a fuller account of the Act and the circulars which have over the years determined local authority practice see LCSS (1977), especially Chapter 2.

Unfortunately it is not clear from the CRC report how many of the minders used by the mothers they interviewed were in fact unregistered. But the authors do demonstrate by means of a careful working through of national figures for 1971, that unregistered ones could not *possibly* exist in anything like a ratio of 10:1. The most it could have been at that time was 2:1.

The beliefs persist, whether or not they are true, both that there are huge members of unregistered minders, and that their care is worse than that of the registered. The authors of a recent report by the Trades Union Congress (TUC 1977) accepted the guesses that have been made and wrote,

> It is . . . variously estimated that between 100,000 and 500,000 additional children are with unregistered childminders.

On 1975 figures this would make the ratio of unregistered to registered something between 1:1 and 6:1, so the estimate has been slightly scaled down from Brian Jackson's version. Jack Tizard and his colleagues (1976) stated simply that it was 'known' that 'most minders' were not registered. An example of that belief, by now a part of public opinion, in the dubious if not scandalous nature of unregistered minding appeared in a headline quoting the chairperson of a newly formed local Childminding Association in the Oxford Journal on 18 March 1977: 'Working mothers are placing their children at risk by placing them with unregistered childminders.'

Here a group of registered childminders seem to have been trying to get the public to distinguish between them as legal, and the unregistered ones, presumed to be offering inadequate care.

Who Minds?, the report published by the Community Relations Commission, added a new dimension to all this concern in pointing out the disproportionate numbers of ethnic minority mothers of under-fives forced to go out to work and yet unable to find what they regarded as satisfactory provision for their children. Black, white and Asian working mothers were interviewed in Manchester, Lambeth, Leicester and Slough.

> Childminders were used by one in three Asian and black mothers, but by only a sixth of white mothers. One in three white mothers used a day nursery, and one in ten a nursery school. In contrast, less than one in fifteen black and Asian mothers had succeeded in finding a day nursery place or a nursery school place, although many mothers stated such provision as their first preference.

The CRC report also quoted a finding, from the small study of multi-cultural minding in Paddington, that non-English-speaking children were often left with minders unable to speak to them in their own language, and who regarded their own methods of child rearing as 'better' than the parents'; this might have effects on the children's feelings of identity and self worth.

Thus, particularly in the early and mid seventies child-minding was seen as 'a problem', although as a problem it was not unique to Britain. In May 1976, for example, an article appeared in the French newspaper *Le Monde* on *nourrices gardiennes* (childminders) who were said to be looking after some 500,000 to 600,000 children under the age of three. The article described a similar system of registration to our own, and recorded disquiet about countless thousands of children thought to be in the care of unregistered minders. The authors also believed that as many as half the children would have changed minders several times by the time they were three. A report from New Zealand, *Brought to mind*, (Julian, 1977) echoed the same concerns. And in the United States a similar view was gaining currency. For example, Donald Peters of Pennsylvania State University wrote in 1972:

> Pines (1966) reported a series of anecdotes of children being neglected or abused by untrained, drunken or sick day care workers [minders]. Pines also reported that

among New York City unlicensed homes, 34 per cent lacked play materials of any kind, 25 per cent never took the children out of doors, and 84 per cent of facilities were rated as inadequate because they violated health codes or because the children were seriously neglected.

Peters also pointed to the belief, and a small amount of evidence to substantiate it, that at its best, minding could be a good form of care.

Focus on the positive

Partly as a reaction to all this, and also perhaps partly as a result of a changed climate of opinion following the oil crisis and cuts in public expenditure in the mid-seventies, there seems to have been a shift of emphasis nationally in the way professionals have viewed childminding.

First, there has been a great deal of work done by local authorities to build up support and training programmes, based on the beliefs that minding is here to stay, has a positive side to it, and is susceptible to improvement. The LCSS (1977) report, *Childminding in London*, begins by saying that one of the two main reasons for its study was concern at the focus of the national discussion prior to 1975 'on bad practice rather than on the positive contribution childminders make to day care for the under-fives.' And at the end, they write,

> The childminding situation reflects the problems of the child of the ordinary working mother: there is a need to rethink the whole of day care provision for the under-fives and to recognize that childminding is a positive part of this.

Not just in London, but all over the country, various local authority social services departments really began to do something about their childminders. We have already mentioned some of the more innovative projects, often mounted in partnership with other organizations. Melanie Phillips writing in *New Society* in May 1976 (Phillips, 1976) shows how rapidly they began to develop services on their own in the twelve months between 1974 and 1975. She gives figures showing that outside London only 13 local authorities were offering services in addition to registration and inspection in 1974, whereas the number had increased to 34 one year later. The kinds of services being developed were mainly courses and informal discussion groups, followed by toy libraries. A few local authorities had started more radical day-fostering or sponsored-childminding schemes. Under these schemes specially selected minders were employed directly by the local authority to look after, mainly, 'priority' under-fives, either as an alternative to day nursery provision or as a complement to it.

The local authorities taking action were still in a minority, of course, but nevertheless a new trend was beginning. In 1977 there was help from an unexpected quarter, in the form of a BBC television series, *Other People's Children*, 20 short programmes aimed at minders. The series was accompanied by a handbook distributed free to every registered minder in the country, and also a set of tutors' notes since it was hoped that individual local social services departments would set up groups using the programmes as a focus for discussion. The BBC had decided to take the initiative in stimulating local authorities into action, raising the morale of minders and getting them to think more about their activities.

Also in 1977, the Association of County Councils and the Association of Metropolitan Authorities brought out their report, *Under Fives: A Local Authority Associations Study*, (ACC/AMA 1977) which made favourable noises about childminders, not unlike the London Council of Social Services report, and argued for the extension of training facilities for them.

Following hard on this, the British Association of Social Workers published its own discussion paper on the under-fives (BASW, 1978), taking an even more positive tone:

The advantages of childminders in providing care for young children are both obvious and subtle. Minders are usually more flexible than day nurseries and they are often nearer the child's home.

Childminders are already providing a significant and important service. Their potential has only just begun to be recognized.

It went on to recommend that

local authorities be urged to increase their input in the field of childminding, with particular reference to support for minders, provision of toy libraries, equipment in the home, etc. . . .

The almost universal assumption behind all this activity and report writing has been that the more 'support' services the local authorities provide for minders, and the more they try to train them, the better will be the care experienced by minded children. This assumption, based – it appears to us – more on faith than on actual evidence, is particularly clear in the LCSS report, which assumes that educating minders is a 'good thing', and considers evidence that minders neither want it nor feel they need it as a challenge rather than a possible indication of barking up the wrong tree. Thus:

Courses for childminders pose a number of challenges, particularly because childminders may be reluctant to go on a course. Experience has shown that attendance is often irregular. Frequently the most regular attenders are the highly motivated minders already offering relatively good child care. Although many minders find they do enjoy group discussion and learn from it . . . , most of them are mothers who may feel they do not need to learn about bringing up children.

A second aspect of what we have called a new focus on the positive side of minding has been an argument put forward in several influential quarters in favour of the minder as a mother figure, offering all sorts of advantages which, by implication, the nursery nurse in a day nursery cannot. The most striking example of this promotion of minding that we have come across is the agreeable picture painted by Pamela Thayer (1976), Principal Social Work Service Officer at the Department of Health and Social Security, with whose words we began this chapter.

> A particularly positive aspect of day care in a family is the opportunity that it provides for the child to make the close, personal, continuing relationships that are so essential as the foundation of sound emotional development. For many children these relationships will be compensatory because these children have missed consistent care in their own homes and the opportunity to learn to relate, to learn to love and be loved and to discover a positive sense of their own personal value.

She praised the local nature of minding, and she went on to say:

> A further recommendation is the opportunity it presents for a wide variety of daily experiences of the world around the child and the opportunity to grow up in an adult world and share adult experiences. And from the parents' point of view, not only can good childminding offer a flexible arrangement with varying hours to suit their needs, and sometimes overnight care, but it can offer local support to parents, particularly to single parents.

Lady Plowden saw minding in a similarly rosy light. In her paper presented to the Sunningdale conference on 'Low Cost Day Provision for the Under-Fives', she talked about minders as a 'resource' (along with mothers, voluntary bodies and statutory bodies) saying:

> My third resource . . . are the proxy-mothers – childminders, who can give a young child that continuity of relationship in a homelike atmosphere within the community that is so important to his development if his own mother cannot care for him during the day.

The view of minders as mother substitutes is again put forward, very forcibly, by the writer Penelope Leach. In *Who Cares?* (1979) she writes:

> Overall I see day minding as the pattern for the future, wherever a child requires non-residential substitute mothering outside his own home.

A third and obvious element in this more positive view of minding has been the fact that in a time of national cutbacks in public services minding is, from the government's standpoint, by far the cheapest form of provision for the under-fives. Brian Jackson wrote in his Sunningdale paper:

> With childminders, no basic buildings are required. They operate from their own home. With childminders, no expensive professional training is needed. It is a matter of modest group discussions, short one-hour courses, regular visiting. We do not want three-year courses at a Royal College of Childminding. With childminders, no expensive kitting-out is needed. It is a matter of modest help – toys, books, play equipment, fire guards.

And the Local Authority Associations' Study which, as we have seen, took a favourable view of minding, aims, very much in the same spirit, to help local authorities improve their services to under-fives *within* existing resources.

It is noticeable that the focus on positive improvements, seems to coincide (if one makes an allowance of a few years after 1971 during which these departments presumably addressed themselves to higher priority problems and groups, and generally settled down after a long period of reorganization) with the transfer of responsibility for minders to social services departments. Faced with the need to get on with the job, it is this stance that local authorities and social workers seem to have taken. Perhaps a certain disillusionment growing up around this time amongst social workers with care provided by day nurseries has also played its part.

This outlook is not just confined to the local level. It is

equally noticeable in policy documents coming out of Whitehall. For example, the joint circular letter sent by the Departments of Education and of Health and Social Security to local authorities in January 1978 lists what the Departments consider to be the advantages of minding as a form of care. They make various recommendations about what local authorities can do to effect improvements – such as passing on names and addresses of minders and minded children to health authorities, so that 'health surveillance' (presumably by health visitors) can be maintained. From this document, the official position seems to be that, in its favour, minding is or can be (a) local, (b) flexible (c) the nearest substitute to the child's own home (d) an opportunity to form 'close, continuing relationships' and (e) better than day nurseries for 'many children under three and those with special problems'. Its chief defect is seen to be that

> children who are *merely minded* (our italics) are more likely than other children to be denied the social and intellectual stimulation that is important to their development.

But the circular assumes that this can be remedied by better 'support and advice services, including in-service training' and other measures. From another corridor of power emerged a report on *Services for Young Children with Working Mothers* (CPRS, 1978), prepared by the Central Policy Review Staff (the 'Think Tank'). Although dealing with services for children up to the age of ten its main emphasis was on under-fives and the provision that should be available for those whose mothers work. After considering all types of care for children in this age group, the report said:

> For the 400,000 under threes with working mothers, trained and supported childminders are at their best and are by far the most economical form of support . . .

The emphasis throughout was on the relative cheapness and efficiency of minding as a service.

Yet another document, this time from the Equal Opportunities Commission (EOC, 1978), discussed day care facilities and opportunities for working parents. While on the face of it the authors did not appear so wholeheartedly in favour of minding

> . . . the standards of care currently provided by child-minders give serious cause for concern and the pay and working conditions of the minders themselves are unacceptable . . .

they went on to add:

> These deficiencies in the minding system can be removed through the professionalization of childminding and the employment of minders by local authorities.

Re-emphasis on concern

However, this newly accepted wisdom – that minding is potentially a very positive form of care in that it provides the nearest substitute to being at home with mother – has not gone unchallenged.

In *Minder, Mother and Child*, Berry Mayall and Pat Petrie of the Thomas Coram Research Unit describe their detailed study of the quality of care given by 39 registered minders living in London (Mayall and Petrie, 1977). They came to the conclusion, after interviewing the minders, observing the interaction between 27 children and their minders, comparing it with the interaction between the same children and their mothers, and also, incidentally, interviewing the mothers, that the minders were *not* acting as mother substitutes, and that the children did not even seem to be 'attached' in the sense that Schaffer and others used the word (Schaffer, 1977). They pointed out that whether it was desirable for minders to be mother substitutes was itself open to question, but found it disturbing that there was so little involvement at all. We do not know how typical their minders were, since they were not randomly sampled and came only from four inner London boroughs. We do know, however, that none were unregistered and the authors were of the opinion that they represented the best minding facilities in those areas:

> The sample of minders which we eventually obtained seemed to us to be in many respects a favoured one. We saw no minders living in bad housing conditions and for the most part their accommodation was clean and well kept. Nearly a third of them (12) had had some work experience relevant to childminding. . . . In addition, more than two thirds of the minders (27) had contact with a special social worker who devoted himself or herself to childminder support or training. Because of this quite a large proportion (60 per cent of the total sample) had taken part in some sort of training scheme.

They felt seriously concerned about the children they observed, who were assessed as not doing well for their age, and in most cases backward on a test of language development. By implication they felt this was due to the minding, although it may not have been.

> The children spent a low-level, under-stimulated day in unchanging, often cramped surroundings. Many did not get the love and attention they needed. Some had experienced frequent changes of minder. Most of the mothers were not satisfied with the standards of care offered.

The fact that a large proportion of these minders had attended specially mounted courses and were receiving above average services from their Social Services Departments of course presents a particular challenge to the idea that the way forward is to provide more courses and support. Jack Tizard argued the irrelevance of training in his paper given to the Sunningdale conference, based on the findings of the Thomas Coram Research Unit:

> Most childminders do the job for their own convenience – and often short-term – because it fits with their domestic commitments, not out of informed, caring interest in children. The very poor rates of pay are an indication of their low and exploited status, and of the residual nature of the job. . . . So training schemes carried out by local authorities are unlikely to affect the attitudes of those currently minding, who have nothing to gain by improving the way they 'mind' children.

The working party of the Trades Union Congress in its report, *The Under Fives,* (TUC, 1977), supports the conclusions of the Thomas Coram study and goes even further in its recommendations for changing drastically the current state of affairs:

> The Working Party recognize that these proposals are far reaching and go well beyond suggestions now being made by some groups, which believe that childminding can be transformed into an excellent service with a few modifications to the existing regulations and servicing facilities. Our view is that the present childminding service is so seriously deficient that only root and branch reform can hope to achieve standards which are satisfactory. . . . We are strongly of the opinion that those who believe that childminding can provide for the nation a good child care service on the cheap are gravely deluded. If the service is cheap it will not be good, and if it is to be made good we can see no way in which it can remain cheap. It is cheap at present only because minders are exploited. We are sure that to advocate a continuation of this system, or a modification of it, is to ignore the needs of the children and we believe it is shameful to do so.

What parents have thought about minding

Parents have probably been largely unaware of the professional debate, except for occasional mention on television or in the newspapers. Nevertheless they have been voting fairly clearly with their feet, and we now have some research evidence about their preferences and their satisfaction with existing services.

Several studies have shown that for parents, childminding is on the whole a relatively unpopular form of care. Most recently Margaret Bone (1977) in *Preschool Children and the Need for Day Care*, gave figures showing that nationally minders looked after only 3 per cent of all under-fives in 1974. While this was one per cent more than children who went to day nurseries, it was still a much smaller proportion, say, than the 18 per cent who went to playgroups. Moreover only 3 per cent of all users of all types of provision gave minding as their first preference.

In a report on demand for preschool provision in Harrow we find that out of 98 mothers of three- to five-year-old children, *none at all* preferred minders, not even the four who were using minders at the time, all of whom would have preferred nurseries. Only six out of a total sample of 205 mothers with children under five, nearly one quarter of whom went out to work, were actually using minders (Harrow, 1975).

In addition, those who do use minders tend to be slightly less satisfied with them than users of other forms of care. In Bone's study mothers were asked in a number of ways about their satisfaction, and she concluded:

> On all but one of the aspects covered mothers of children with childminders were no more likely than others to be critical of the facility. . . . The exception concerns the value of the experience for the child, and in this case rather more of the children with childminders than other users had mothers who doubted that the arrangement was good for them. It may be that what

worries most of the mothers concerned is the popular stereotype of childminders, rather than any bad experience of the arrangements for their own child.

She may be right that this is an effect of the mythology surrounding minding rather than an indication of anything real: certainly there seemed to be no significant difference on dimensions like whether the mother thought the child enjoyed going. Nevertheless mothers using minders were less happy with them. The mothers in the Thomas Coram study seemed to be fairly dissatisfied too: 'Nearly half the mothers wanted a complete change from the minder for their child.'

This contrasts rather strikingly with the picture one gets from reading about the recently improved Danish system of childminding. The Wagners describe the popularity and growth of this system as 'extraordinary'; they cite as evidence waiting lists, and growing demand – particularly of parents of 'average' (as opposed to 'at risk') children (Wagner and Wagner 1976). In Denmark there seems to have been a really substantial commitment by the state to minding as a 'quality' service, though even here there are reports of returning doubts, and the whole system is now once again under review.

There is some circumstantial evidence that by and large parents choose minders only as a last resort. According to Brian Jackson (1976), upper- and middle-class parents have not made much use of minders, preferring such alternatives as *au pairs* and nannies. He says

> childminders tend overwhelmingly to serve those children whose working mothers are poorly educated, poorly skilled or in very disadvantageous circumstances. The Community Relations Commission inquiries illustrate the abnormal importance of childminding in the immigrant community. Similarly one can illustrate its major place in the lives of single-parent families, or generally show it to be a function of working class life.

The LCSS (1977) adds:

> A number of local authorities responding to our own questionnaires said that a large proportion of the people using childminders were those with low incomes.

In the areas where the Community Relations Commission carried out its researches (1975),

> childminders were used by one in three Asian and black mothers, but by only a sixth of white mothers.

The mothers interviewed by Mayall and Petrie also fit roughly into this general category, although a surprisingly large proportion were classified as in non-manual occupations; just under half the sample were immigrants:

> Of the men they were married to, or living with, three were unemployed, five were students, four were engaged in non-manual work and the rest (12) in manual occupations. . . . Twenty-three of the mothers [out of 27] were employed in non-manual work. The large proportion of mothers who fall into the III non-manual group (15) were doing the sort of work which is fairly typical of working women in London; they were clerks, shop assistants and shorthand typists.

It comes as a surprise, then, to see that in a national study (Bone, 1977) of a random sample of 2,500 under-fives, this view is not, in the main, borne out. Childminders did *not* seem to be used most by working class parents, *nor* did they seem to be used most by the lowest paid. In fact Bone concluded that neither social class nor parental income made any difference to the type of provision used. But minders *were* used more by mothers of children under two, presumably because of a lack of alternative options:

> Use of childminders, day nurseries and crèches did not appear to be related to age, but because use of other forms of provision was quite rare before the age of two use of childminders formed a relatively high proportion (40 per cent) of all use amongst these youngest children.

The reason for the discrepancy between the findings of this national sample and the other impressions and findings we have quoted may perhaps lie in the fact that these have all been concerned predominantly with large urban areas, and not with the national picture. We know very little about minding in areas where it has not been viewed as a problem.

It seems likely that it is viewed much more positively in some areas, for example possibly in stable working class areas not suffering from inner-city problems. In small towns and rural areas it could well be viewed differently by parents, and indeed be operating differently. There is some evidence from the United States that lends credibility to this hypothesis. The Peters (1972) study of minders in the state of Pennsylvania compared minders living in low, medium and high density areas, and concluded that minders in the highest density urban areas had 'the least adequate environment, the most negative atmosphere', and were 'the most under-equipped'.

But back in England, the fact seems to be that more and more parents are using minders, whatever their feelings about them. Although, as we have said, there are problems interpreting the figures available from the Department of Health, whatever figures one accepts as valid there has been a clear growth in both the numbers of registered minders and the numbers of places available from 1949 up till now. For example, the BASW (1978) report shows 26,300 registered minders in 1975, and a rise to 28,700 just one year later. It is possible that some of this growth reflects a movement from unregistered to registered minding: there is no evidence either way. It is also theoretically possible that it represents only an increasing *desire* to mind, rather than an actual increase in minded children: it may be that more and more women are applying to become childminders but not actually succeeding in finding any children to mind. But against these two considerations we must weigh the increasing trend, year by year, for mothers of under-fives to go out to work – while the number of State day nursery places fails to grow. *Either* all these extra under-fives are being taken care of by fathers and other close relatives, *or* there must be a real increase in the numbers of children being placed with minders, or both. It seems most likely to us that parents *are* turning to them more and more.

How minders have seen themselves and their work

Very little has been written about how minders view themselves.

These are women working in isolation in their own homes and until very recently they have not begun to form into groups or make their views known. Nor, until the last few years, has there been much research on the question.

The earliest opinion we have come across was that expressed by Monica Artis, who formed the Sutton Child Minders' Action Group and wrote in a newsletter in 1974:

> Until childminding is seen not as a problem but as an opportunity, the problems we face cannot be solved. Until the childminder knows intuitively she is part of the pattern of child care, (i.e. as a social worker rather than something to be solved by a social worker) she will naturally react with suspicion and apathy to all moves from above to improve the quality of child care. (Quoted in LCSS, 1977).

This is a very acute view of how minders were viewed at that time – and of how they would prefer to be viewed.

In the Thomas Coram study, Mayall and Petrie asked a series of questions designed to find out how the minders saw their job, and found

> the prevailing impression received from the answers to these questions . . . was of a casual approach to a job which provided a bit of pocket money while fitting in with the minder's main preoccupations: her domestic commitments and personal situation.

In fact they did not really regard it as a job at all. The picture gained from this study does not differ in essence from the one the authors quoted from Dickens's *Our Mutual Friend,* written well over a hundred years ago –

> 'Those are not his brother and sister?' said Mrs Boffin.
> 'Oh, dear no, ma'am. Those are Minders.'
> 'Minders?' The secretary repeated.
> 'Left to be Minded, sir. I keep a Minding School. I can only take three, on account of the Mangle. But I love children and Fourpence a week is Fourpence . . .'.

Neither does it differ in essence from the picture Donald Peters found in Pennsylvania:

> The vast majority of home mothers saw themselves as baby-sitters and not as having any major responsibilities for the education or development of the children in their charge. For many the work was not even considered as a legitimate paying job.

But it could be that the minders interviewed by Mayall and Petrie were in some way atypical of minders in Britain today. Several observers have suggested a difference between committed, or vocational minders on the one hand, and casual or temporary ones on the other, and it could be that the Thomas Coram minders fell predominantly into the second category. The authors of a short report on childminding in the county done by Cornwall Social Services Department in 1974, saw the minders they talked to as follows:

> It seems reasonable to divide the childminders into two categories – the transitory and the potentially 'professional'. Of the nine minders interviewed, six were in the first category and only three seemed to have long term potential as a reliable day care resource.
> One of the most striking characteristics of the latter three minders was their attitude to the mothering of their own children – all stated quite clearly that one of

the prime reasons for becoming minders (as opposed to finding paid work outside the home) was a determination not to deprive their own children of their full-time attention . . . In marked contrast, all six transitory minders expressed the intention to take employment outside the home as soon as their own children started school.

We take up this possibility later, in our own study.

At any rate there seems to be a striking contrast between the way the Thomas Coram minders seem to have seen their 'job' and the way minders in the newly emerging associations are talking now. Now that a self-help movement is growing among minders, and local associations and pressure groups are being formed all over the country, along with a newly formed National Childminding Association, the impression we get is one of keenness and dedication. To give just one example, Anita Burchall, a childminder from the Gillingham Childminders Association is quoted in the second newsletter of the NCA *Who Minds?*, which came out in February 1978:

> As a newly registered minder I was shocked to find out that my image and that of my fellow childminders was not as nice and respectable as I thought. Alright, so there are some bad minders, but please don't tar us all with the same brush. . . . An attitude that annoys us is the them-and-us, i.e. working mothers and childminders. What do the people who comment think we are? Are we less than mothers because we *choose* not only to stay at home and look after our children, but other mothers' children?

If some minders are finding the energy to form groups, attend meetings, contribute to newsletters, campaign for courses and toy libraries, and so on, there must be, one would suppose, at least a proportion who like their work and want to improve the service they give.

What does all this add up to?

Out of this mass of conflicting opinion, assumption, fact and myth, what can we say with any certainty about childminding and childminders?

Childminders are used almost exclusively to care for the children of working mothers, although there is a growing tendency for children who are defined as 'at risk' and in need of day care to be placed with minders too.

The extent of minding is very difficult to calculate; a small proportion – 3 per cent – of under-fives is involved. But by 1976 that accounted for as many as 65,000 children minded full-time by registered minders, many more minded part-time, and an unknown number in the care of unregistered minders.

Minders are used by parents of all social classes, but are not a very popular form of care; most parents, given the choice would not initially opt for a minder.

Minders themselves feel undervalued and criticized by society and are taking steps to dispel their poor public image and achieve recognition for the job they do.

These are fairly uncontentious statements, but beyond them everything is open to doubt. Although it is asserted that being minded is like being at home with mum, there is little evidence that it is, or even that it is desirable that it should be. However, enough different people have recorded high turnovers of minders and children, cramped and unstimulating environments, overminding and slow development of children, to raise serious doubts about its merits as a form of preschool care.

Local authorities, supported by central government, recognize that the service needs to be improved and are beginning to experiment with selective registration, training, both pre- and in-service, and support schemes. But there is no evidence that any of this helps the children: that in changing minders' attitudes and their self-image, it also changes their behaviour towards the children – and their parents.

Much is made of the economic advantages of minding; it is said to be a very cheap form of care. There is no doubt that as it is practised now, this is true. Hardly any public investment is required. And for the ordinary working mother, whose chances of a free day nursery place are in most areas negligible it is the cheapest available. Minders' pay, on the other hand, is derisory. There has been only one serious attempt to assess the cost of a salaried, well staffed and equipped childminding service (Willmott and Challis, 1977), and that showed the cost differential between day nursery provision and *that* kind of minding to be marginal.

When we began our own study, then, we found no real evidence on the merits of minding from the point of view of minded children, only evidence casting doubt on it. But at the same time there was a growing enthusiasm for minding and pressure for its expansion as *the* form of provision for the future. We therefore set out to examine some of the main issues, hoping to throw light on some of the assumptions, beliefs and recommendations we have described.

2
The setting of the survey

In this and following chapters we describe a survey of childminding in Oxfordshire which we carried out in 1977. The choice of venue for this survey was a pragmatic one which had little to do with minded children since the survey was only one of several studies of preschool children undertaken by the Oxford Preschool Research Group, including work in local nursery schools and playgroups. However, it is often agreeably possible to make a virtue of necessity, and there are a number of things about Oxfordshire which make it an appropriate choice. Foremost among these is that it stands, as we shall see, in marked contrast to the deprived inner areas of large cities where most previous studies of minding have been concentrated.

How typical is Oxfordshire?

Oxfordshire is largely a rural county: there are few towns of any size: the largest are Oxford in the middle, and Banbury in the north. Both of these have at least one large industrial complex. Other smaller towns with established industry include Witney and the railway town of Dicot. Otherwise the country is chiefly agricultural, and the proportion of economically active employed in agriculture is 38 per thousand, twice the national average.

Generally speaking, though, Oxfordshire is a county of moderation, if not well-heeled, than at least not barefoot. It has a fairly low rate of unemployment at 3·6 per cent of the population. Its housing standards are quite good: only 10 per cent of households lack at least one of the three basic amenities – hot water, inside lavatory, and fixed bath, compared with 18·4 per cent in the country as a whole and approaching 50 per cent in some London boroughs. Similarly, overcrowding is quite slight with only 5·2 per cent of households having more than one person per room compared with 6·6 per cent nationally and over 10 per cent in many London boroughs. Looking at car ownership, one of the few variables available from the *Census* which indicates wealth, Oxfordshire also compares favourably with 14·2 per cent of households owning two or more cars, as against 8·4 per cent nationally and under 2 per cent in Tower Hamlets.

These figures are drawn largely from a DHSS report 'A classification of the English personal social services authorities' (1977), which groups together local authorities which show similar patterns of social need using 23 variables. In this analysis Oxfordshire comes in Cluster 1, a large cluster of non-metropolitan counties, suburban metropolitan districts and outer London boroughs. 'These authorities are typified by being fairly close to the average in most variables and by being below average in those most indicating social need. In particular *they have proportionally fewer one parent families than most other authorities and a comparatively low number of working women with children under five years of age*' (our italics).

While it has a comparatively high proportion of preschool children (84 per thousand of the population), Oxfordshire actually has the lowest proportion in England of mothers with children under five working more than 30 hours a week: 17·9 per cent compared with 31·3 per cent in the country as a whole and 56·0 per cent in Haringey. It also comes well down the list in the proportion of single-parent families, ranking 83 out of 108 local authorities; 7·5 per cent of families with children being lone-parent families, against a national average of 9·4 per cent and over 15 per cent in five London boroughs.

These two characteristics, the low proportions of full-time working mothers with preschool children and of single-parent families, ought between them to result in a low demand for full-day care and little pressure on resources.

This would suggest that Oxfordshire minders may be less in demand than in some other areas, and therefore less likely to be taking large numbers of minded children. Thus the mothers who use them may have a greater choice of minders. We may, therefore, expect to find a more favourable picture of minding than has been found so far in areas such as the inner London boroughs, which persistently emerge as areas of high social need.

Nevertheless we should not forget that averages over one local authority can conceal considerable variation within it, and there could have been hidden pockets of high social need within Oxfordshire.

The official position

When we began our study in 1976 it would not be unfair to say that relatively little was being done by the county to encourage minding, and that the prevailing attitude tended towards the 'children-are-better-off-at-home-with-mother' position. This was also evident in the very low provision of day nursery places: there were three day nurseries, two in Oxford City and one in Banbury, which provided 95 places altogether for a potential population of about 40,000 children – about two places per thousand children. However, in the provision of nursery schools Oxford City in particular had a long and impressive record.

After the local authority boundaries had been redrawn in 1974, a working party was set up 'to review the provision in new Oxfordshire of preschool facilities for children 0–5'. Their report, entitled 'Beginnings', dealt with minding at some length, and discussed in detail the problems and advantages of this form of care. Five main recommendations were made:

1 That registration of childminders (and playgroups) should be the responsibility of a member of the Social Services staff specializing in the care and well-being of children under five.

2 That childminders should be visited at least every six months and a written report kept of each visit.

3 That childminders should not be responsible for more than three children under five years including their own children.

4 That a panel of specially selected minders acceptable to both health visitors and Social Services should be set up to take on the care of babies who would otherwise be cared for in day nurseries. These minders would be paid for by the local authority.

5 That opportunities be made available for childminders to meet each other and to attend courses. These courses might be ones already set up for parents and playgroup workers or they might be specially arranged. The possibility of financial help to enable minders to attend was also envisaged.

In 1974 when the report was written this all looked encouraging and enlightened, but it was soon overtaken by the national tide of economic recession and inflation, and never officially adopted as policy. Only the first of the recommendations, concerning specialist staff, got anywhere near implementation, and, since the package as a whole was intended as much for playgroups as for childminders, this cannot be seen as a decision to invest heavily in childminding as a service. The recommendations about numbers of children to be minded and about opportunities for minders to meet, since they cost little, made some progress.

By the time of our survey, therefore, the county's support for childminders was small. The Social Services Department had divided the county into eight areas: six of these had part-time workers, and one a full-time worker, responsible for both playgroups and childminders. The remaining area divided responsibility for minders between two social workers, leaving another staff member to deal with playgroups. They came from different professional backgrounds, some from nursery schools, some with child care qualifications, some from playgroups and some from social work. They worked as members of their area social work team, although most did no active casework as such. In other words, if problems arose in a minded child's family, none of these social workers would normally be involved. Their job was to register playgroups or childminders or both, and to support and develop these services by giving advice, considering training needs, and generally being available.

Beyond this there was little going on. A few priority children were placed with minders. Occasional coffee mornings or evening discussion meetings were organized in two areas. There had also been a brief skirmish with a toy library, but this had petered out through lack of interest and difficulty in reaching minders spread over a rural county. One specialist worker who asked to spend the money allocated for toys on training instead was refused.

There was however one venture on the part of the Social Services which arose out of the BBC television series *Other People's Children*. This went on the air in January 1977 after an intensive campaign to persuade local authorities to use it as a basis for training minders. In Oxfordshire a small amount of money was made available for specialist workers to bring minders together to watch and discuss these programmes, and in three areas some discussions did take place. These coincided with the planning stages of our research, and we were able to participate by observing some groups and getting others to complete questionnaires.* While only a tiny minority of the county's minders were involved, there is no doubt that the whole enterprise did have some effect, and resulted, much later, in some minders setting up permanent groups and in two areas starting up local associations.

The survey: aims and methods

In the light of what we knew of the county our starting point for the survey was relatively optimistic. We expected to find that minding in Oxfordshire would be different from that in

* For a full description of this, see *Television and Childminders* (SSRC, 1978).

large cities such as London, and that this difference would generally be in the direction of better housing, fewer children per minder, fewer language problems between minders and children from different countries, more part-time minding, better local facilities such as parks and open spaces, better local networks of relatives and friends to support the minders, and so on. On the other hand we expected minders to be less well supported by the Social Services Department and to have little contact with specialist workers other than when they registered.

We also expected that minders in Oxfordshire would be just as underpaid and apparently exploited as minders in large cities: indeed, perhaps even more so if we were right in predicting a low demand for minders and a shortage of children to mind. Equally we had no reason to think that Oxfordshire minders would be different from large-city minders in their attitudes to minding or their understanding of the needs of young children, and we expected to find – as in any group of individuals – a range of good and bad care for minded children.

What did the survey aim to discover?

Broadly our aims were twofold: first to describe how minding worked in Oxfordshire and whom its main users were, and secondly to examine the quality of care being provided for the minded children. We also intended to look at unregistered minders, but this was not in the end possible. We will consider each of these aims in more detail.

How minding worked

The sorts of questions we wished to answer were: How many registered minders were actually minding children, were still potential minders or had given up minding altogether? How many years they had been minding and how long did they intend to continue? How great was the turnover among minders? Why did minders start and stop minding? How did the system of registration work and what role was played by the social services? What numbers of children of different ages were minded and for how many hours a week? What were the minders paid and how was it decided? What expenses were involved in minding? How were minding arrangements set up and ended? What sorts of people took up minding in terms of their age, family composition, social class, education, training, and previous patterns of work, and how did they differ in these from the mothers of minded children?

From the mothers we also wanted to know what their original preferences had been for care for their children; how they found minders and decided they were suitable; how they combined work with bringing up young families; whether their children had been to other minders or to other care-takers previously, and so on. We concentrated on mothers rather than on both parents since it is usually the mother who takes primary responsibility for the care of the children.

The quality of care

In addition to describing how the service worked, we also wanted to investigate the quality of care which the minders were giving the children. This is a much more difficult aim, and one which cannot easily be encapsulated in a series of questions and answers, but the sorts of areas we were interested in were: the opportunities for play and explora-tion, and for making friends with other children and adults; minders' understanding of the needs and feelings of young children in general, and the quality of their relationships with particular minded children; their attitudes towards working mothers in general and their relationships with particular mothers; how they dealt with problems over the child's routines, health, speech and behaviour.

Unregistered minders

Our third aim was to try to locate a group of unregistered minders and to compare them with the registered ones. We had planned to do this by picking one small area, perhaps situated near to a factory or other institution employing large numbers of women, which we would then search by various means for unregistered minders. However this sort of exercise is very time-consuming, and in the end we could not fit it in. We feel this is a very unfortunate omission in any study of childminding, because we have no way of knowing whether unregistered minders exist in large numbers or whether, if they do, the children in their care are receiving worse care than those with registered minders.

The few attempts that have been made to investigate unregistered minders suggest that some fail to register through ignorance of the law rather than through any intention to flout it. Certainly a number of minders in our survey had started minding without realizing at all that they were supposed to register. We also found that the mothers using minders tended not to have relatives nearby, and it seems likely that other mothers using unregistered minders would in many cases be using relatives. Neither case seems to fit the stereotype of the unregistered minder herding large numbers of young children into damp and dangerous basements.

However we did come across one mother in our survey who had been an unregistered minder for children of friends and acquaintances (she was cheaper than others nearby), and she had been discovered by the health visitor with twelve children in one room all listening to pop records. So clearly the problem does exist, to however small an extent. On the other hand we also found large numbers of registered minders who wanted to mind but who could not find children to look after, and with such an abundance of choice it does seem unlikely that many mothers would allow their children to remain in grossly overcrowded, deprived or dangerous conditions. Yet mothers, too, may be ignorant of the law, and the abundant choice may be more apparent than real if there is only one convenient minder, registered or not, in the same street.

The sample of minders

Our sample of minders was randomly selected from the lists of registered minders kept by the Social Services Department. Separate lists were kept for the eight administrative regions, and within these for individual towns and villages. The lists contained approximately 460 names and addresses, and from these we drew a two-in-five sample of 182 names. Of these, 68 turned out to be currently minding one or more children ('active minders'), 75 were not currently minding but were available to mind ('inactive minders'), and 26 were no longer available nor interested in minding ('ex-minders'). Thirteen could not be contacted or traced. Of these, eight had moved away, and the remaining five were not found at home after repeated visits. A further four, two active and two inactive minders, declined to participate in the study. This left 165 (91 per cent) who were subsequently interviewed, 66 active, 73 inactive and 26 ex-minders.

The sample of mothers and children

Our only means of obtaining the names of minded children and their mothers was from the minders themselves. That meant that they could not be randomly selected from the total population of minded children and mothers in the county, but only from the children attending the sampled minders. There were 98 of these children, and since they included seven pairs of siblings, there were 91 mothers. Just under half the children were 'singly-minded', that is to say they were the only minded child with that minder, and the rest were 'multiple-minded', usually with one or two other minded children.

Since we could not interview all the mothers, we selected one child and mother from each minder using random selection tables. This meant that our sample was biased towards 'singly-minded' children, since we included all of these, 46 altogether, but only 20 of the 52 'multiple-minded' children. We could not know in advance what effect this bias might have, but there were reasons why it might be important. Were we, for instance, over-representing 'better' minders? It could certainly be argued that minders with only one minded child might find it easier to develop a close relationship with the child, and to give him more attention. Also, no minder with only one minded child could be said to be minding primarily for monetary reward, given the low rates of pay.

In order to check on possible bias we collected some information on all 98 children. This showed that by and large the sampled children did not differ significantly from the excluded children. However the sampled children tended to be younger (52 per cent were under three compared with 33 per cent of the excluded children), and we shall see in later chapters that younger minded children fare somewhat better on some measures than older ones. The sampled children also differed significantly from the excluded children in how they came to be with their minder: 40 per cent of the sampled children were with their particular minder because their mother and that minder already knew each other, and only 8 per cent because another mother had recommended the minder. These figures compared with 20 per cent and 38 per cent respectively of the excluded children. One would expect that arrangements set up on the basis of pre-existing friendships might have favourable consequences for the child, but in the event it did not seem to be an important factor when we came to analyse the data. It would probably be fair to say, however, that any bias in our selection of children and mothers was probably working in the minders' favour rather than to their discredit.

Another way of dealing with our sampling bias was to weight the data. This is a statistical procedure which involves giving unequal weights to the individual data based on the initial probability of each child being selected. While the statistical ramifications of this procedure need not concern us here, one practical advantage is that it makes a technical correction for bias, and allows more confident generalizations from the sample to the population as a whole. This is perhaps best illustrated by an example. The unweighted figure for cases where mother and minder were already friends, was 40 per cent. The weighted figure was 32 per cent, while the figures for all the 98 sampled and excluded children was 33 per cent. So the weighted figure gave a much better approximation to the true distribution.

One disadvantage of weighting is that it is confusing, since mysterious totals appear which do not correspond to actual numbers of people. We have therefore limited its use largely to the overall demographic characteristics of the mothers in our sample, since, in any case, there were very few differences between children minded on their own and children minded with others.

Of the 66 mothers selected, 63 agreed to be interviewed. Four of these were actually fathers – three whose wives had left them and one who, though married, was effectively the main caretaker of their eighteen-month-old baby. With some reluctance we decided to lump these fathers under the majority category of 'mothers', in order to avoid both the clumsy repetition of such phrases as 'mother or father' and 'her or his' and also the ambiguous 'parents' which may mean one parent or both.

By the same token we decided to refer to the minded child as 'he' to avoid the constant irritation of 'he/she'. Although there was an equal number of boys and girls, we felt that among the largely female cast in this book the masculine gender would help to distinguish the child from 'she the minder' and 'she the mother' (despite the four who were 'he the mother'!).

How minders and mothers were contacted

We first sent the minders a letter explaining the aims of the survey and informing them that a member of the research team would be calling during the following week to arrange an appointment. The letter also stated that they need not feel they had to see us if they did not want to. We were fortunate in having the full cooperation of the Oxfordshire Social Services Department, and were able to enclose a statement from the Director informing minders that his Department supported the aims of the research and hoped they would agree to take part.

An interviewer then called on the minder to give a personal explanation, to find out how many children were being minded and select one of them, and to fix up a convenient time for a full interview on a day when the selected child would be there. While this preliminary visit probably increased our travelling time and expense, we felt it would be unfair to expect people looking after small children suddenly to make a couple of hours available without warning. And it may well be that this extra effort in setting up the interviews had something to do with the fact that so many minders agreed to take part in the survey. Minders who were not currently minding were usually given a short interview there and then, since this only took about 15 minutes.

We used exactly the same procedure to contact the mothers. The interviews were arranged during the daytime and, wherever possible, at the same time of day and within a week of the minder's interview. The reason for this timing was that we would see the child on both occasions in similar states of tiredness, and would cover roughly the same events in his life. For mothers working part-time this was relatively easy, but those working full-time had to be seen at weekends. Occasionally the gap between the two interviews turned out to be rather more than a week.

How the information was collected

The questionnaire

The main method of collecting information from minders and mothers was by means of a structured questionnaire composed of specific questions. The answers were not, for the most part, precoded, but were written down verbatim. While the interviewer was generally expected to follow the order and wording of the questions, she was allowed to be flexible within specified limits, and was expected to use her own judgement in pursuing points raised by the informant.

Diary of 'yesterday'

In order to get a feel for what the minder's, mother's and child's day was really like, part of the interview was spent on going through the previous (or most recent) day in great detail. We started at the point when the minder or mother had got up in the morning and finished for the mother when she had gone to bed, and for the minder when the minded child had left. We recorded to the nearest quarter hour where the adult and child were in relation to each other, what they were doing, and whom else the child was with.

This technique has been used quite widely with children, and has been found to be quite reliable (Douglas *et al.* 1968). It has advantages over asking about a 'normal' day, in that detailed questioning of actual events is thought to break down synoptical qualities of these events and to minimize unwitting distortion. It has the disadvantage that 'yesterday' may sometimes be very untypical, but this untypicality can be explored, and over a number of interviews it evens out – some days being much more complicated, others less, than usual.

Observations and ratings

In addition to asking for specific information, we treated the interview as an opportunity to observe the behaviour of the minded child towards his minder or mother and vice versa, because we felt the quality of their relationships would be as much revealed by what they did as by what they said. It has been shown that direct questions about attitudes and feelings are of dubious validity, and that observation of actual behaviour, including for instance tone of voice and facial expression, may be more informative. It has been shown, too, that the frequency of interactions and of responses to them, and the expression of warmth, hostility, and so on can be reliably observed and rated (King *et al.*, 1971; Rutter and Brown, 1966).

Similar sorts of observations had been made on minded children in London by Mayall and Petrie, and we decided to repeat some of their methods so that we could make direct comparisons of minding in the two areas. We therefore took as our observation period the first 20 minutes of the interview. We felt this period had certain advantages. Firstly it was a time when all the children would be in a similar situation of having to adapt to the arrival of a stranger and to the subsequent loss of attention. Secondly it was long enough to allow the children to get used to us, but short enough to avoid prolonged frustration for the child.

During the 20 minutes we recorded on the questionnaire all approaches which the child himself initiated to his minder or mother. Approaches were defined as any of the following: touching; crying or shrieking accompanied by a glance towards the adult; speaking to her; showing her things; coming within a yard and looking at her. Where the minder had a child under five years of her own present, we also recorded his approaches to her. If she had more than one, we selected the one nearest in age to the minded child.

Immediately following the end of the observation period the interviewer completed a set of ratings aimed at summing up the child's behaviour – mostly actual events, including where he moved to or what he did immediately on the interviewer's arrival; his mobility, from being strapped in a pram to moving about and actually leaving the room; whether he interacted or actually played at least once with other young children present, and what he spent most of the time doing.

During the rest of the interview we recorded whether the

minder or mother touched the child affectionately at least once, including whether she caressed, cuddled, kissed, patted or picked him up. We also counted the number of positive or negative remarks she made about him, and rated her warmth towards him on a five point scale. Our definitions of these took into account not only the content of what was said, but also the tone of voice in which it was said and other non-verbal behaviour such as facial expression.

In a concluding section of our observations and ratings – one having nothing to do with behaviour – we asked to see all the toys provided at home and at the minder's. We then made ratings of the presence or absence of toys in a series of specified categories: construction toys, books, noisy toys, riding and climbing toys, and so on. We also rated them on five-point scales for quantity, quality, variety, accessibility, age appropriateness, and for whether they were sorted and usable or all jumbled up.

Reliability

In order to test the reliability of our observations and ratings, we carried out a number of joint interviews. As in most research projects which have to be completed within a couple of years, there is never enough time, and we were not able to test for reliability in as much detail as we should have liked, but 16 interviews were carried out by pairs of interviewers, each of the four interviewers interviewing and observing with each of the others. The interviews had to be used both for discussion about disagreements and as tests of reliability, since we did not have time to do a second set of pilot interviews, and consequently our final level of agreement was almost certainly higher, following our discussions and clarifications of definitions, than the results we give below would suggest.

The warmth ratings turned out to be quite reliable, with 94 per cent within one point and 50 per cent absolute agreement. There was no difference between interviewers and observers, nor, as far as we could tell from small numbers, between different pairs of judges.

The ratings of positive and negative remarks about the child were not tested for reliability at the time, but we followed the definitions used by other workers which have been shown to be reliable (Caldwell, 1967). Judgements about whether tone of voice conveys positive feeling, which is part of the definition, are virtually the same as judgements of warmth, and so we have no reason to think they were any less reliable than our warmth ratings, but we can be less sure about negative or hostile remarks. However we discussed between us any doubtful ratings.

Paired ratings for the child's behaviour during the observation period were only available for five interviews, so it does not make much sense to talk about percentage agreement. On three ratings, the child's first response to the interviewer's presence, the dominant activity and whether the child interacted or played with another child present, there was agreement in four of the five cases. There were only two agreements on the child's mobility, but this turned out to be because of different decisions about whether L-shaped, open plan living areas and kitchens counted as two rooms or one, and not actual disagreements about where the child was. We originally had a fifth rating – 'the child's involvement with his environment' – but this turned out to be very unreliable and we had difficulty in agreeing on what we meant. We therefore decided not to use it.

The toy ratings had good reliability on the whole. Decisions about the presence or absence of toys in each category were made jointly for ten of the interviews, and 93 per cent of these were in absolute agreement. The differences were all to do with allocating the same toy to different categories, for example, whether tricycles used indoors and out should be under 'riding and climbing' or 'outside' toys, and we resolved these by more comprehensive definitions. The other toy ratings were done on nine interviews and were less reliable. Taking them overall, since the amount of agreement did not vary much between them, 31 per cent of the ratings were exact agreements, but 90 per cent were within one point difference. In view of the latter we decided to collapse the five-point scales into three-point ones, which gave us 74 per cent absolute agreement and 91 per cent within one point. On individual scales, accessibility, variety and age-appropriateness had the highest agreement, eight out of nine for the first and seven out of nine for the last two.

The presence of other adults during the interview

In the majority of the interviews the minder or the mother was the only adult present, but in 39 per cent of the minders' and 41 per cent of the mother's interviews a relative or friend was present for some of the time. Also the interviews done in June and July coincided with a period of industrial action by Oxfordshire teachers, and in a few of these the older children were sometimes present as well, since they were unable to go to school.

We had expected that the presence of other people would affect the child's behaviour in the observation period, and had originally intended to leave these children out of the analysis. However, when we compared those interviews carried out with others present and those carried out without, there did not seem to be any differences between them in, say, the number of approaches the child made to the minder, and since our numbers were not large we decided to leave them in.

This, then, was the background to the survey, and these the methods we used. In the next five chapters we give the results, starting in Chapter 3 with a look at who minds and who uses minders.

3

Who were the minders and mothers?

Some women stay at home and look after other people's children: others leave their children with minders and go out to work. Why? Is this a matter of choice, habit, conviction, necessity, custom or what? In this chapter we shall try to answer this question by looking at the backgrounds of these two groups of women and at the reasons they give for their decisions.

Throughout the chapter we shall include among 'minders' all the 165 active, inactive and ex-minders, but also look for differences between them. We have some reason to think that our category of 'inactive' minders may have contained some minders who had really given up and become 'ex-minders'. Over a third of them had actually found a job, and a small group had turned a child down in the last six months on the grounds that they were not taking any on at the moment. On the other hand they may have gone back to work *faut de mieux* because they could not find a child, and we shall see that interesting differences do emerge between 'inactive' and 'ex-minders' which would support the overall validity of the distinction.

Among the 'mothers' we shall include the three lone fathers, in spite of the fact that the social pressures on men to go out to work are quite different from those on women. We do this because we are interested in the forces which bring *all* minded children to minders, and also because we felt the fathers could have chosen to give up work and care for their own children. Some fathers do decide to do this, and indeed one of our three fathers said he still would do so if he felt his children were unhappy. Occasionally, where it would make nonsense of the data to include them, we shall leave the fathers out, for example, in considering the age at which mothers have their first baby.

Their families and previous life experiences

Age and family

The first thing we can say is that the minders were significantly older than the mothers. Most of the minders were in their thirties, as can be seen from Table 3.1, while most of the mothers were in their twenties. Secondly, the minders were more likely to have lasting marriages than the mothers. Only 3 per cent of the minders were divorced or separated as against 18 per cent of the mothers, and a further 4 per cent of mothers were single. Two minders and one mother were widows.

Age group	All minders		Active minders		Mothers	
	Number	Percentage	Number	Percentage	Number	Percentage
−20	0	0	0	0	1	1
20–29	52	35	22	33	32	57
30–39	85	58	35	53	27	42
40–49	23	14	7	11	3	5
50+	5	3	2	3	1	1
Total	165	100	66	100	64*	100

* Weighted data

Table 3.1 *Age of minders and mothers*

Thirdly, their own families were quite different. While all but one of the minders had children, their children were considerably older. Only half the minders had a preschool child, but about half had children of primary school age compared with a third of the mothers, and half the minders had children of middle and upper school age compared with only a fifth of the mothers.

Not only did the minders have older children, but they had more children as well (see Table 3.2). Half of them had three or more children, as against only a tenth of the mothers. One obvious explanation of this is that the minders are older, and therefore closer to having completed their families. However, this may not be the whole truth. Nearly a quarter of the active minders had four or more children, which seems very high when we consider that the proportion of married-couple families with four or more children in the county is only 4·4 per cent (and only 4·2 per cent in England as a whole). This may suggest that minders have, and want, large families and enjoy having children around.

	All minders		Active minders		Mothers	
	Number	Percentage	Number	Percentage	Number	Percentage
0	1	1	1	2	0	0
1	15	9	9	14	32	50
2	77	47	24	36	21	33
3	44	27	17	26	7	11
4+	28	18	15	23	4	6
Total	165	102	66	101	64*	100

* Weighted data

Table 3.2 *Number of children*

Perhaps supporting these speculations, the minders had started their families significantly younger than the mothers: the mean age of the active minders when they had their first child was 22 years 6 months, as opposed to 24 years 8 months for the mothers. And quite a high proportion of minders had either adopted children or become foster mothers (21 per cent), while only one mother had adopted a child (this information was only available for active minders).

'Rootedness'

We expected that the minders would have more local roots in their areas, have lived there longer and have more of their extended family around, than the mothers. One reason would be that mothers who had relatives nearby would probably leave their children with them rather than with minders. However, we also thought that women who had grown up in the area and had a local network of relatives and friends might feel more supported and relaxed at home with young children and less in need of getting out to work.

While we had expected such a network, we had not anticipated its extent, which seemed remarkable. Four fifths of the minders had lived within five miles of their present address for more than five years, half for more than ten years, and a third for more than twenty years – or virtually all their lives. In marked contrast to this, over half of the mothers had lived in the area for five years or less. Detailed figures are given in Table 3.3.

	All minders		Active minders		Mothers*	
	Number	Percentage	Number	Percentage	Number	Percentage
Less than 1 year	1	1	0	0	6	9
1–5 years	28	17	8	12	27	44
6–10 years	54	33	20	30	13	21
11–19 years	29	18	16	24	7	12
More than 20 years	51	31	22	33	9	14
Total	163	100	66	99	62	100

* Weighted data

Table 3.3 *Number of years in the area*

Similarly minders were twice as likely to have their own parents or siblings living within five miles of them: half the minders had at least one relative, and often many more, nearby, compared with only a quarter of the mothers. It is interesting, however, that this difference was not found for the ex-minders: while they had lived in the area for just as long as other minders, significantly fewer, only 16 per cent, had a relative close by.

Social class

Looking at the husband's occupation we once again found significant differences between minders and mothers, with mothers tending to be of a higher social class. Two thirds of the mothers on whom this information was available had husbands in non-manual occupations compared with only one third of the minders. As we can see from Table 3.4, the social class of the minders' husbands did not differ markedly from Oxfordshire as a whole, except that rather more of them were in skilled manual jobs. By contrast, half the mothers' husbands were in social classes I and II (professional and intermediate), twice as many as in the county generally. However, only 2 per cent of minders or mothers had husbands in unskilled jobs (social class V) just one third of the County average.

We also looked at social class as measured by the minders' and mothers' own occupations, although the Registrar General's system of classification is not very satisfactory for women's jobs. Basically the picture was much the same, as can be seen from Table 3.5, although the differences were smaller. This was largely because the minders' jobs,* compared with their husbands', were more in the skilled non-manual sphere, no doubt reflecting the high number of service and clerical jobs done by women.

It is clear, then, that minding is not, as some have suggested, a service provided by and for working class mothers. On the contrary, minders come proportionately from all social classes except the lowest one, while the mothers who use them tend to come disproportionately from the upper echelons, at least in Oxfordshire.

Education, qualifications and patterns of work

Not surprisingly in view of all these differences, minders and mothers also differed in their education and higher qualifica-

---

* Taken as the job with the highest social-class status of any they had previously held.

	All minders		Active minders		Mothers		Oxfordshire†
	Number	Percentage	Number	Percentage	Number	percentage	Percentage
I Professional, etc.	11	7	7	11	10	16	6·7
II Intermediate	22	13	7	11	17	27	19·6
III Non manual	23	14	6	9	8	13	11·1
III Manual	71	43	31	47	13	21	32·9
IV Partly skilled	31	19	13	20	4	6	21·0
V Unskilled	3	2	2	3	1	2	6·8
No husband/ unclassifiable	4	2	0	0	10	16	1·9
Total	165	100	66	101	63*	101	100

* The three lone fathers have their own occupations entered here, not that of their wives.
† Figures from the 10% sample of the 1971 Census: occupations of economically active males excluding those in armed forces.

Table 3.4 Social class: husband's occupation

	All minders		Active minders		Mothers	
	Number	Percentage	Number	Percentage	Number	Percentage
I Professional, etc.	5	3	3	5	4	6
II Intermediate	38	23	17	26	27	43
III Non manual	62	37	21	32	16	25
III Manual	17	10	9	14	9	14
IV Partly skilled	34	21	12	18	5	8
V Unskilled	6	4	3	5	1	2
None/ unclassifiable	3	2	1	2	1	2
Total	165	100	66	102	63	100

Table 3.5 *Minders' and mothers' occupations**

* Registrar General's classification of occupations.

tions. In the first place minders spent significantly less time in school: nearly two thirds left school at 15 or earlier, compared with under a third of the mothers; and two fifths of the mothers stayed at school until 18 as against only 6 per cent of the minders.

After school these differences inevitably persisted. Three fifths of the mothers went on to get further qualifications and 15 per cent took university degrees: under a third of the minders had higher qualifications, and under 2 per cent had degrees.

Their previous patterns of work were also different. Although, like the mothers, the minders had almost all worked full-time outside the home on leaving school, they had usually stopped doing so at marriage or the birth of their first baby. Half of the minders had reduced their hours and worked part time after this point, and a further 41 per cent had stopped going out to work altogether; only 8 per cent had continued full-time. In contrast, half the mothers had stayed in full-time work, and most of the rest continued to go out to work part-time. Only five mothers did not go back to work at all.

While the majority of minders had left school early and without formal qualifications, quite a number of them had experience or training relevant to their work as minders. We include here such things as nursery or infant teaching, nursery nursing, playgroup training, residential child care training, or other work in any of these fields, or as a nanny in a family. We found that 38 per cent of active minders had had some such training or experience – which was interesting in itself. Even more interesting, though, was that this was not true for the inactive and ex-minders where significantly fewer, only 16 per cent, had such training or experience.

It is tempting to conclude from this that parents were looking for and choosing minders with some apparent expertise in child care beyond their experience at raising their own families. However we shall see in the next chapter that mothers do not give this as a criterion for selecting a minder, and, indeed, that they do very little selecting of any sort, rather tending to take the first minder they come across.

There are a number of alternative explanations. One is that the minders with relevant training or experience are more interested in children and therefore make greater efforts to find children to mind; but again we did not find much evidence that most minders, active or otherwise, put themselves out to find children. Perhaps, then, the mothers who used them liked them and recommended them more to others, or perhaps the specialist workers or health visitors tended to pass their names round more. Whatever the reason, it might seem fortunate; yet, as we shall see later in this book, we did not find any evidence that these minders were any 'better' than other minders.

Why mind? Why go out to work?

Having seen how different the lives and families of minders and mothers are, we now turn to the reasons they give for deciding to stay at home and look after other people's children or to go out to work. Our interest is not so much in comparing minders with mothers, since we would not expect reasons for decisions of such opposite types to have much in common, but in looking for differences within each group: for example, between minders who have given up and those

	Active minders		Inactive minders		Ex-minders		All minders	
	Number	Percentage	Number	Percentage	Number	Percentage	Number	Percentage
Less than 6 months	4	6	2	3	3	12	9	5
6–23 months	22	33	17	23	11	42	50	30
2–5 years	25	38	41	56	10	38	76	46
6–10 years	9	14	9	12	2	8	20	12
More than 11 years	6	9	4	6	0	0	10	6
Total	66	100	73	100	26	100	165	99

Table 3.6 Length of time minding

who are still minding; or between mothers who have a professional training and career and those who do not.

There are two things we must keep in mind. The first is that when we asked for reasons we left the questions open, so that the answers were entirely what minders and mothers raised spontaneously. We hoped in this way to get at what they themselves felt to be the important motives behind their decisions, rather than prejudging the issue by providing them with possible answers. It means, however, that we cannot assume that if they did not mention something they did not feel it. Not giving a reason is not the same as answering 'no' when asked directly.

The second thing to remember is that we were asking about decisions made in the past, and for some of the minders, especially, the quite distant past, so their answers have to be interpreted in the light of hindsight. How much hindsight can be seen in Table 3.6 which shows when minders first took up minding. For example, nearly a fifth of the minders had made their decision more than five years ago.

Why mind?

The minders' most frequent reasons for taking up minding were centred not surprisingly, on their own young children.

	Percentage giving this as a reason*		
	Active minders	Inactive minders	Ex-minders
Love of small children	36	32	15
Company for own child	18 ⎱ 45	25 ⎱ 50	39 ⎱ 58
Didn't want to leave own child	27 ⎰	25 ⎰	19 ⎰
Money	26	16	23
Bored, needed other interest	15	12	15
Started as a favour, to help mother	30	33	46
Total minders in this category	66	73	26

* Percentages total more than 100 since some gave more than one reason.

Table 3.7 *Reasons given for starting to mind*

As we can see from Table 3.7, about half either said they did not want to leave their own children or said they wanted to provide company for them.

The next most frequent reasons, each given by about a third of the minders, were either that they did it to help out a friend or that they loved having small children around. These two reasons were rarely given by the same minders, and may well, therefore, discriminate two rather different types of minder, those who drift into it because it is convenient for them and others at the time, and those who do it out of a more general interest in children. The natures of their answers are best conveyed in some examples:

> Her mum came and asked me . . .

> I think a friend asked me and it just sort of happened.

> . . . to oblige a friend of mine.

or

> I adore babies and I fell for her.

> I love children – I wasn't happy if I wasn't with children, minding or fostering – for instance, holidays we enjoy through the children; it keeps us young.

If they *are* two distinct groups of minders, one would predict that the first kind, those who do it to help out one particular mother and child, would be less likely to carry on once that arrangement had ended. If we look separately at the ex-minders we can see that this may very well be so, since they were the most likely to give this reason and by far the least likely to mention love of children. Moreover all but two of them, as we saw in Table 3.6, had given up minding within five years and often considerably sooner. So it may well be, although we cannot know, that a number of the active and inactive minders, about a third of whom had also given helping out a friend as a reason, would also give up within a relatively short time – and indeed perhaps some of the inactive ones had in effect already done so.

The only other reason which figured at all frequently was money. Given the very low rates of pay which minders were getting, we were surprised that so many did mention this – about a fifth of all the minders and over a quarter of active minders. However we shall see in a later chapter that minders did not on the whole see minding as a job, but rather as a source of welcome pin money which they could spend on 'extras'.

We can say finally about their reasons that very few minders saw minding as a solution to boredom at home or as giving them another interest over and above being a house-wife and mother. Since an extra child to look after is likely to add to rather than detract from what turned out to be, as we shall see in Chapter 5, an already astonishingly busy domes-tic routine, there is no real reason why they should see it this way. Nor do we have any particular evidence that they felt bored or depressed at home, although one minder had been recommended by the health visitor to become a minder in order to avoid being depressed, and there were a few whom we felt at the interview were rather dejected and lonely.

In any case, at the time they made their decision to become a minder the majority of them did not see them-selves as having the alternative option of going out to work. Four fifths answered 'no' to the question 'Was there anything else you might have done?' Indeed we would not have expected most of them, coming from close-knit, deeply rooted, semi-rural and probably middlingly prosperous fami-lies, and with inclinations towards large families of their own, to be women eager to throw off their 'domestic shackles'. On the contrary, they emerged as women whose first and unequivocal priority was to stay at home with their children, and they were often unsympathetic to the idea of other mothers going out to work. Eight per cent of the active minders were highly critical of mothers leaving their young children, 38 per cent were less extreme but generally against, and while 55 per cent were more positive, even these tended to give only qualified approval.

The ex-minders, in contrast, did not appear to be so

unequivocally committed to staying at home with their young children. Although, like the other minders, when they first took up minding they did not see work as a viable possibility, by the time we saw them a good many seemed to have changed their minds. Two fifths of them still had a child under five, and over half of those who had were already back at work full- or part-time – that is, over a fifth of all the ex-minders. There were suggestions that the ex-minders generally seemed to have a lower tolerance of being at home. Four fifths of them were working out of the home, over twice as many as the inactive minders. All of them said there were things about minding which they did not like or enjoy, again twice as many as the active and inactive minders. And over a quarter of them complained of feeling tied to the house – yet again twice as many as the other minders. Four ex-minders said they found minding unstimulating or depressing.

Why go out to work?

We now turn to the mothers. As we have seen, not only do they have young children, but they are more likely to be single or living alone after the break-up of their marriage, and to be without supporting relatives living near them; they

	Number	Percentage*
Needed money	31	57
Bored, lonely, fed up (or wanted to prevent that)	21	35
Love job, wanted to 'keep hand in'	16	27
Never actually stopped	13	22
Therapeutic reasons	7	11
Wanted to study	4	6
Wanted to stop/avoid drawing social security money	4	6
Other	10	17

* Percentages total more than 100 since some mothers gave more than one reason.

Table 3.8 *Mothers' reasons for going back to work (excluding those who were not working mothers).*

also have a higher level of education and better qualifications than minders, and often have professional jobs and careers. All these things in different ways make it more likely that they will want or need to get an outside job, whether through lack of money, loneliness or interest in their work (see Table 3.8).

And these were the three reasons the mothers gave most frequently in answer to our open question: 'What made you first decide to go back to work after having a child?' By far the most pressing concern, mentioned by over half the parents, was money. The following are examples of the sorts of things they said

'I had to – money; no other reason.'

'. . . the money; I don't think you can manage these days on just the one wage.'

'Finance . . .'

'We wanted to buy our own house . . . that was the only way we could get enough for the mortgage.'

We did not ask for family income, but inferring that the lower the occupational status the lower – very roughly speaking – the income, we found that women with husbands in manual occupations were more likely to give money as a reason. Rather to our surprise the single mothers were no more likely than the married ones to say they were working for the money – although four of them did say they were doing it in order to avoid having to draw social security payments, which they found distasteful.

A reason almost as pressing as money, and mentioned by over a third of the mothers, was that they felt bored and lonely at home. A further 11 per cent mentioned more specific 'therapeutic' reasons such as feeling 'down', 'depressed' or 'blue', or the stress of looking after very difficult children. It would seem, then, that nearly half were finding being at home with a young child a difficult or dispiriting experience, one which their own words can convey much better than ours:

> I got into a rut – I got sick and tired of looking at four walls.

> My husband's always been on nights and I was getting fed up, so I thought I'd get a job.

> I was bored, and lonely . . .

> I don't like staying at home, I don't think it would be good for me and the family if I was at home all day.

> . . . to get away from her [the child], she was very difficult . . . on the go all the time, my mother had to come round because I couldn't cope with her, she never slept . . .

Recent work on the causes of depression has shown that a job outside the home can protect women from becoming depressed in the face of stress, especially women with several young children and who lack an intimate relationship with a husband or a confidante (Brown and Harris, 1978). It would seem, then, that some of our mothers may have done the sensible thing in deciding to go out to work.

A third fairly common reason, mentioned by over a quarter of the mothers, was that they liked their work and wanted to keep their hand in so as not to get out of date in their chosen field. These women tended, not surprisingly, to be the ones with better qualifications and higher occupational status, working perhaps as teachers or doctors. For some of them the money they earned was not all that important, not as important, anyway, as the rewards of work they found satisfying and stimulating, and quite a high proportion of them worked part-time as we shall see.

The choice of job and hours

As well as the actual decision to work, other decisions have to be made about jobs and hours, and arrangements to be made for the children. Some of these decisions will depend on mothers' reasons for wanting to work in the first place. For example, a single mother who needs money will probably need to work full-time, and this may outweigh other considerations such as the congeniality of the work. And other consequences will follow from the need to work full-time: for example, her choice of care for her child will be limited to whatever can cover her long hours. At the other end of the scale, where money is not the chief motivation to work, the content of the job may be very important, as may be the decision to work part-time or full-time. The option of part-time work will also be related to the type of work; for example, it is not very easy to find part-time factory work, and some of the largest employers in Oxfordshire, such as British Leyland, are very reluctant to take on part-time women.

So 'choice' may not be quite the right word for some mothers whose circumstances largely dictated how they ended up. And a fifth of the mothers did not have to choose a job, since they went back to ones which they were already in and which were held open for them. We can see from Table 3.9 that nearly all of the mothers in professional and intermediate jobs stayed in the same job or the same line of work after having their baby. However about half of them

		Number	Percentage
Continued with previous job/career/training (Social class I or II*)	full-time	13	21
Continued with previous job/career/training (Social class I or II*)	part-time	16	25
Continued previous job/type of job (Social class III, IV, V*)	full-time	11	17
Continued previous job/type of job (Social class III, IV, V*)	part-time	1	2
Took any job	full-time	6	10
Took any job	part-time	10	16
Other, not working		6	10
Total		63	101

*Registrar General's classification of occupations.

Table 3.9 *Mothers' decisions about jobs and working hours*

reduced their hours and worked part-time. This did not happen at the lower occupational levels, where only a third of the mothers in skilled, semi-skilled and unskilled jobs continued in their previous job or line of work, and only one mother did so part-time. It would seem that these mothers, especially if they wanted to reduce their hours to be at home with their children, had to be prepared to accept a change from, say, factory work to shop work, and to take what they could get.

The choice of care

Finally we come to the question of child care; what arrangements did mothers want for their children, and what did they get? Discussing events in this order implies that they occurred in this order, but of course life is not like that and in some cases parts had to be fitted together like a jigsaw; there was no orderly series of events. A mother who thought about working may have had a friend round the corner who offered to take the child if she found a job; she might even have suggested it, knowing the mother to feel under pressure at home and feeling it would be good for mother and child to be apart for some of the time. 'It just happened', or 'I always knew she'd take him if I got a job', were not untypical responses. However there were other mothers for whom there was no obvious caretaker to hand, and who had to search around once the job was settled.

We asked mothers what type of care they had *originally* wanted for their child when they first went back to work, so their answers did not necessarily refer to their current circumstances – for instance they may have been living in another area or the child in question may have been an older sibling of the one in our sample. There are other reasons, too, for interpreting their answers rather cautiously. The question itself was somewhat ambiguous; it could be interpreted as an 'ideal' choice in the best of all possible worlds or a 'pragmatic' choice within the bounds of what they knew to be available.

Moreover it is quite likely that the different day care options were not clearly understood by everyone. For instance 'day *nursery*' and '*nursery* school' are sometimes confused. So, too, is the non-existent 'playschool': both halves of this word occur in different forms of care, and it can be used to mean either '*play*group' or 'nursery *school*'. Indeed there is evidence of widespread confusion even among those who compile official statistics on day care provision (see Smith and Harris, 1978). Fortunately, though, the one we are most interested in, 'childminder', is the least ambiguous.

We can see from Table 3.10 that two fifths of the mothers gave a minder as their first choice. In view of all our notes of caution we can, perhaps, infer that this is a maximum, and may include some mothers who might have liked a day nursery but knew that they had virtually no chance of finding one in Oxfordshire.

	Number	*Percentage*
Minder	24	38
Day nursery	12	19
Playgroup	6	10
A relative	5	8
Crèche	4	6
Nursery school	4	6
Other	3	5
No preference: 'it just happened'	5	8
Total	63	100

Table 3.10 *Mothers' original preferences for care*

In fact, the mothers in our survey did not differ significantly from mothers nationally in their preference for minders. In a national survey of families with children under five years, 29 per cent of mothers using minders said they preferred them (Bone, 1977). If we allow for the fact that Bone had a separate category of mothers (14 per cent) who said they did not want their children in day care at all (i.e. mothers who were compelled by circumstances to work), the two surveys may actually be even closer.

So we can say that the majority of the mothers in our sample had not originally wanted a minder, and would have preferred some other form of care for their child. Over half of these did try to find what they wanted, but about half of them again were unsuccessful. Some did manage to get what they wanted, and turned to a minder only when that arrangement fell through. For example, one mother had her child in a day nursery in another area, but could not find a place when she moved to Oxfordshire; another, with an Oxfordshire day nursery place, was told that costs were to rise sharply the following week. A third mother, who had chosen a relative to care for her child, quarrelled with this relative and found herself seeking an alternative at a day's notice.

Thumbnail sketch

To end this chapter we shall give quick portraits of a minder and a mother of a minded child, based on the differences we have found. If any minder or mother reading them finds them to be too arbitrarily standardized, let us hasten to say that they are intended only to highlight the differences and not to do violence to the rich variety of individuals we met in the course of our interviews.

A minder

We can characterize the minder as being married, in her early thirties, with three or possibly four children, and quite likely a foster child too. Some of her children are already in school. She has lived in the same area for most of her life, and has parents, brothers or sisters living nearby. She left school at fifteen and went more or less straight out to work until her marriage or the arrival of her first baby, after which she stayed at home or perhaps worked part-time. At some point she may have worked with children.

She has married a man who is in skilled or semi-skilled work, and they are still living together. She feels little stress at being a mother and housewife, and is strongly convinced that she should stay at home with her children at least until they start school. Indeed she may be rather unsympathetic towards mothers who leave their young children and go out to work. She also thinks her children would benefit from the company of other young children, and since she enjoys having small children around she decides to take in minded children. If she is not especially interested in children and does not have training or experience in child care, but simply agrees to help a friend by taking in her child, or, if she does not have relatives near her, she may stop minding and go back to outside work.

A mother

The mother of a minded child is very different, and although in some respects all the mothers resemble each other, in others they seem to form two rather distinct groups – but still quite unlike the minders.

The mother is probably younger than the minder by about three years, and has only one or two children, who are still very young. She was not brought up in the area but moved there fairly recently, and she does not have her parents or siblings living close to her. She stayed at school until she was 17 or 18, and went on to get higher qualifications. After this she worked in a relatively high status job and continued working full-time after her marriage. Her husband's occupation is also high status. She started her family later than the minder. She finds being at home with a young child frustrating and unstimulating, and sees a job outside the home as an antidote to misery or depression. Or she may want to give her family some of the good things of life, or continue a career which she finds stimulating and rewarding. She is not overkeen to leave her child with a minder but does not have much choice among forms of care.

Alternatively, her marriage may have broken down, and she may be the main breadwinner. In this case she may work full-time and have a less enjoyable job.

So we have on the face of it a situation where the interests of minder and mother would seem to coincide felicitously, where both Jack Spratt and his wife may be satisfied. However there are already in this chapter a few danger signs that the dish is not entirely to the taste of either; that it may be soured for the minder by her hostile feelings about the mother having left her child, and for the mother by her knowledge that she would have preferred some other arrangement for her child.

In later chapters we shall see again how conditions appear rather satisfactory; minders and mothers able to organize their lives without too much apparent stress, and children enjoying comfortable surroundings with plenty going on to occupy them. And yet we shall also find increasing cause for unease emerging from behind this agreeable and encouraging façade.

4

Minding arrangements: how they work

How do mothers and minders find each other? How do minders register, and what does this involve? How do mothers decide whether a minder is suitable? What sorts of things do they ask each other, and how do they come to an agreement over the details of the arrangement? Once an arrangement has been made, how do they help the child to adjust to this potentially threatening change in his way of life? Do problems arise, and how are they dealt with? Do mothers and minders talk to each other about progress and problems? Finally, what sort of things cause arrangements to break down?

In this chapter we shall look at minding arrangements, and try to answer some of these questions. Since a number of the children had already been going to the minder for a year or more, we felt that the early stages of the arrangements were often too distant in time for information to be very reliable. We therefore picked out a small group of ten children, who had all started in the last month, for more detailed analysis. Our questions about problems, too, were all confined to the last month.

Registration

We start, for convenience, with registration, although this was not always the beginning of the story: quite often minders only applied to be registered when they had already agreed to take on a child, but the great majority, 79 per cent, put in their applications before they actually started minding. However, this leaves a substantial minority who started by minding illegally.

Minders found out about the need to register in a variety of ways, but usually on the grapevine. One fifth had been told by a friend or relative; 17 per cent had picked up the information from radio or television, or had read it in the newspapers; 12 per cent were told by another minder. Some knew because they were already foster parents; others heard from the parents of a minded child. The main 'official' source of information was the health visitor; these visitors had told 11 per cent of minders. Virtually no-one mentioned any social services publicity. Dissemination was clearly a rather haphazard and chancy process.

What was involved in registration? Few minders mentioned filling in the extensive and detailed form, nor having an X-ray, but most remembered checks on various aspects of safety. About half said they were asked to take some precautions beyond those they had considered necessary for their own children: most commonly to buy a fireguard, and less often to blank off electric sockets or install a stairgate. Sometimes we came across rather curious restrictions. For example, one minder had only the ground floor of her house approved, on the grounds that the first floor was a fire risk. This meant that technically the minded child had to stay downstairs; but since he lived in an identical house next door, the minder felt this was rather absurd.

About three quarters of those who were asked to make alterations had done so, even though it had cost a fifth of them more than £5. The rest had ignored some or all of what they were supposed to do.

Registration was not always speedy. While just over half the minders said it had been completed within three months, a third said it took four to six months, and 7 per cent more than six months. One minder had waited over a year. Although we did not ask specifically how they felt about this delay, surprisingly few minders seemed to have been put off by it. Nor did they seem deterred by the investigations that went on, although one minder said she had been 'frightened' by the fire officer's visit and by 'things in the registration papers about going to court'. We cannot know, of course, whether any potential minders were put off altogether, and gave up the idea of minding – or of registering.

One thing that may have helped minders to tolerate the delay was the specialist workers' pragmatic response to those who were waiting to start minding a particular child. One quarter of the minders said they had been told just to go ahead and start without waiting for the registration papers to come through.

For a tenth of our minders their Oxfordshire application was not their first, since if a minder moves into a new local authority area she has to re-register.

We asked minders whether they felt there had been any benefits or disadvantages subsequently in being registered. Over a third could not think of any benefits. The rest felt there were some, most often a comfortable feeling of being within the law; 17 per cent of those who thought there were benefits also saw registration as a convenient way of recruiting new children, because their names were on the social services list, and we shall see that this was an important source.

Few saw any actual disadvantages. The impression we gained was that the whole issue was more or less irrelevant to the minders, except to the extent that they did not want to be outside the law.

The search for children and the search for care

How does a minder find children to care for, and how does a mother find a minder? How much choice is involved on either side, and is the process in fact in any way selective?

How minders found children

We found that, on the whole, minders did not see themselves as finding children, so much as being found. Of the active minders who had vacancies – almost two thirds of our sample – only six were making any attempts to fill them. The rest were content to wait until approached, relying on personal recommendation or the social services list to put them in touch with mothers. The inactive minders, those who had no children at all at the time of interview, took a similarly passive view; only 14 per cent were taking any positive steps to find children. It was, for the minders, much more a question of being available when approached.

Even when approached, minders did not appear to feel under any great pressure to take children on. Most of our active minders had had at least one inquiry during the last six months, and a fifth reported more than five inquiries. Their reasons for not taking on a child were usually that they had no vacancies or did not want another child at the moment, but a few (15 per cent) said they could not manage the hours required by the mothers. We also asked whether there were any sorts of children they preferred not to take; 29 per cent said they would not consider babies under six months old, and 5 per cent said they would not have immigrant children.

As we would expect from the minders' 'waiting for something to come along' attitude, very few of the children currently being minded had come through advertisements, and most had come through some kind of personal contact (see Table 4.1). In a third of cases, the mother and minder already knew each other, and in nearly a fifth another mother of a minded child had recommended the minder. The social services list of registered minders was also a frequent source, and to a lesser extent health visitors also played their part in passing minders' names around.

We can also see from Table 4.1 that the children we selected for special study contained more of those whose mothers and minders were already acquainted and less whose mothers had heard about the minder from a mother of another child going to that minder. This was because the former were more likely to be 'singly minded' children and the latter more likely to be 'multiple minded'. We have already commented on this source of sampling bias in Chapter 2.

	Children selected for special study		Children excluded from special study		All children	
	Number	Percentage	Number	Percentage	Number	Percentage
Mother a friend or acquaintance	26	39	6	18	32	33
Social services list	22	33	7	21	29	30
Another mother recommended	5	8	12	36	17	17
Health visitor	5	8	3	9	8	8
Another minder recommended	1	2	2	6	3	3
Sibling of another minded child	1	2	2	6	3	3
Social services referral	1	2	1	3	2	2
Other (e.g. advertisements in shop windows)	5	8	0	0	4	4
Total	66	102	33	99	98	100

Table 4.1 Source of all present minded children, selected sample and others

How mothers found minders

The mothers' accounts of how they found minders were, not surprisingly, very similar to those of the minders. The main difference was that more mothers mentioned the health visitors, and correspondingly fewer the social services. This may be partly because the distinction is not always clear to many people, and also because the mother's most 'natural' source of official information is her local welfare clinic and the health visitor she already knows. So if the health visitor mentions a list of registered minders it seems very likely that the mother will assume it comes from her office.

The process of selection

Do minders 'select' children as individuals, or do they take all comers provided the hours and so on fit in? We found virtually no evidence, apart from an occasional preference for a child of a particular age or sex, that minders made judgements about the suitability of individual children, or their parents, and only three of the active minders had *ever* refused a child because they did not like either child or parent. It seems that if the hours are likely to fit into the minder's own family routine, this is enough. We shall return later to this tendency of minders and mothers to see children as somehow 'undifferentiated' in, for instance, their lovableness.

Like the minders, the mothers, too, seemed to make very little attempt to 'shop around' and select a minder. For nearly two fifths of our sample, the present minder was the only one they had heard about (this includes some cases where the mother knew the minder already); for most of the remainder the present minder was the only one the mother actually saw, even though she was given several names. Nor did mothers take steps to check up on minders' good characters, whether or not they were already friends. Nearly three quarters made no further inquiries about the minder; one fifth said they asked around informally, a very small number checked with the health visitor or the social services, and only one asked for references.

How then did a mother decide that a minder was suitable? Often there were several considerations, but three quarters mentioned some aspects of the minder's personality; this response is typical:

> It's difficult, how do you decide . . . ? Her children were happy, she was placid and warm.

Another large proportion of comments (58 per cent) centred round the way the minder behaved or related to children, and a further quarter round facilities at the minder's house. Almost all the mothers gave one or other of these reasons, sometimes together with other reasons such as geographical convenience, the minders' availability or her experience and qualifications; these other reasons rarely featured on their own. A few such as those quoted below, felt it was difficult to make a realistic assessment:

> I didn't really . . . I just dumped my daughter with her and that was it . . .

> I didn't . . . I couldn't tell, it's a chance you take.

Some of these comments were made a considerable time after the event, and we therefore looked in more detail at the ten children who had started at the minder's within the last month. Four of these arrangements were between friends, but in the other six the minder and mother had not known each other at all. The picture here was very similar, as the three examples we give below would suggest.

> When I went to see her . . . I thought she was near to my work and near to Michelle's school and she seemed a nice friendly person. [Child aged three years ten months started less than one month previously]

> . . . (she) was the only one there was left in K. . . . I wrote to them all on the list and they'd stopped. [Child aged eleven months; started two weeks previously]

I don't know . . . How can you tell? . . . I don't
think I could tell from meeting for a short time, that's
why I don't bother to go round any more – you're taking
a risk anyway – how can you tell whether your child's
being looked after properly . . . That's why I prefer a
crèche. [Child aged eight months. This one had started
two months previously]

As well as discussing specifically what qualities made them
choose the minders they used at present, we asked the
mothers what sort of person *in general* made a good minder.
For the majority, the most important, overriding, consideration was that the minder had children of her own, and that
she seemed to be a competent mother; this seemed almost
taken for granted in their assessment of their own minder's
suitability.

It was hard to tell how important it was to parents that the
minder was registered. We know that most of them (84 per
cent) knew about registration – although that still left a
substantial minority who did not – and most knew that the
minder they found was either registered or in the process of
becoming so. On the other hand two fifths said they would
have used her anyway even if she had not been registered,
although they may have said this with the advantage of
hindsight, knowing that the procedure was more or less a
formality. Even so, three in five mothers felt that registration
was significant, that it was a sort of '*Good Housekeeping* Seal
of Approval' on the minder's suitability and competence,
and they seemed to attach more importance to it than the
registration procedures would seem to justify. It may be,
then, that registration makes some mothers feel they need
not make too many inquiries of their own about prospective
minders.

The negotiations

Again, the label for this part of the process is in many ways
inappropriate. As we shall see, the setting up of arrange-

ments often seems arbitrary and vague. It was clear that a crucial part of the discussion concerned money. This often appeared to be decided by the mother; directly, by what she offered in 28 per cent of cases:

> [How did you decide what to charge?]
> I didn't, his mother told me how much she paid.

or indirectly, by what the minder thought she could afford, in 13 per cent:

> I look at them and think are they hard up or not. . . .

But a substantial group (23 per cent) had a standard rate, or a rate they believed was standard. A further 13 per cent asked other minders to establish what they charged. Just 6 per cent mentioned Social Services as having offered guidance on this topic. For some (11 per cent) there was an element of negotiation:

> 'You sort of agree between you, discuss . . . '

The whole issue was often seen as awkward or embarrassing:

> Well, that's what I don't like. Some people tell me they charge more. I wish there was a set rate. The father wasn't working at the time.

> She asked me [what I charged] and I said it's up to you so she said, 'No, you decide', so I said, 'I don't like talking about money', so she said she'd give £2 per day.

> I tried to find out at those meetings [what others charged] but it seemed to be something people didn't like to talk about.

In general, the mothers recalled similarly the way in which agreement had been reached, and were also embarrassed. A much larger proportion (58 per cent) thought the minders had a standard rate:

> She said there's a set rate – £1·40 a day including meals.

> She told me what she wanted. . . .

and fewer thought it was dictated by what they had offered (13 per cent) or could afford (8 per cent); but almost exactly the same proportion (12 per cent) recalled some negotiations:

> I don't know . . . we just came upon a figure which was quite reasonable. . . .

Almost a quarter – 15 out of 63 – commented on how low the charges seemed to be:

> I left it to her to say what she thought was a fair amount. I don't think it's enough, quite honestly, but then I'm not in a position to pay any more.

> She had a rate per hour – I don't think it's nearly enough.

> She told me what she was getting previously – it was abysmally low.

> I asked her how much and she said £8 for the two – amazing to me, I had visions of paying about £15.

Rules and conditions

We asked minders and mothers whether the minder had specified any rules or conditions at these preliminary meetings, and once again found nothing that seemed to warrant such a formal label. Most could not recall anything being said. Two fifths of the minders said they had mentioned something, for example, the necessity for mothers to keep to agreed hours and to let them know if the child was not coming, and to pay regularly, but we got the impression that they did not put them forward forcibly as rules. Also some of the things mentioned seemed more to be preferences or even just points of information than conditions.

Even fewer mothers, only a quarter, recalled minders mentioning any rules. This may have been because they had forgotten or because they did not perceive the things minders mentioned as rules, perhaps both. Certainly in the vast majority of cases, 64 out of 66, nothing was put in writing, although six minders were intending to have a written contract in future. And where two minders did have written contracts the mothers concerned had apparently forgotten about them.

Looking at the ten very recent arrangements where both minder and mother ought to have been able to remember what was said, five mentioned no rules. There was some suggestion that in the remaining five the sorts of things mentioned were not exactly rules, and sometimes not very clearly stated, for example the minder who said:

> Only that I don't cook during the day – and I've got four cats.

Information exchanged about the child

As far as we could tell, the information necessary for emergencies was normally exchanged and the minders almost always knew the mother's home address and where she could be contacted during the day. We did, however, come across one minder who knew the mother's place of work but did not know her surname nor what she did – this particular child was prone to bouts of illness requiring emergency hospital treatment. All the minders knew that they should have the name of the child's doctor and a minimal medical history, and some had cards provided by the social services department for keeping this information.

Beyond this both minders and mothers seemed rather vague about what they had initially asked or told the other about the child. Some mentioned sleeping routines or food likes and dislikes, and one minder said she always asked if the child had special words for drinks and so on which she would need to understand. Others said 'Oh, the usual things'. Since many of them may have had difficulty in remembering what was discussed, we looked separately at the ten recent arrivals.

In four of these cases the minder knew the mother and the child already. However, even in the other six cases, recent though the arrangement was, neither minder nor mother reported much:

> MINDER: I just asked was she healthy, she didn't have fits or anything – I always ask that.

> MOTHER: I didn't tell her much – just that she might cry at first and she said she'd try it out for a week to see if Michelle liked it and how it goes.

> MINDER: The mother told me about her going to the toilet – she's prone to threadworm. . . . She told me about what food she likes.

> MOTHER: She's very susceptible to tummy bugs – I told her that.

Even in these recent cases the exchange of information, as reported to us, was very limited indeed. It would seem that apart from some aspects of health, neither saw it as particularly important or relevant. Rather, then, as we saw with the minder's apparent lack of concern over selecting a child she can relate to, it is as though the child is seen not as an individual but as a child who will have or will need all the 'usual things' a child has or needs.

Starting at the minder's

Settling in

Once the arrangement had been agreed on, what happened next? How did the minder and child get to know each other? As we have seen, two fifths of them were already acquainted, although we did not ask whether in these cases the child was used to being left with the person who was to be his minder or knew her house or her own children.

Since these children were over-represented in our sample, it is important to look at the remainder separately. Most of the 40 children who did not know their minders were taken to meet them by their mothers, either when the mother first approached the minder, or subsequently though before they started being minded. Usually, however, this was just one visit, or at the most two. There were occasional exceptions. For example, one mother had taken her child to spend six afternoons with the minder over a period of three weeks and had stayed there with him. In another case, of a very young baby, the minder had come to the baby's house to look after him for a few weeks so that he could get used to her there.

We would emphasize, though, that these were very much exceptions. Most children who did not already know their minder had only a cursory introduction to her before being left with her. Worse, nearly a fifth of them went to the minder on their first day without ever having seen her before. Sometimes the casualness of the arrangements seemed really disquieting. One child started going to both nursery school and the minder's on the same day – and was picked up from the nursery school by the minder whom she had never met before.

In view of all this it is not surprising to find that less than a quarter of the minders thought that mothers ought to stay to settle their children on their first days, while over half definitely preferred the mothers to go straight off. The remainder were unsure.

Nor did most of the mothers stay; 61 per cent went straight off, and many of those who stayed did so for only a few minutes. The minders did not seem to be very successful in persuading mothers to stay; only half the mothers whose minders thought they should stay did so. A more detailed look at the ten recent arrangements confirmed this picture.

The first week

We asked how the child had got on during his first week at the minder's. By and large the minder and mother gave similar accounts, and basically reported very little trouble, but this may have been partly because of the length of time which had elapsed for many of them. However one mother could recall vividly her child's first week which had been almost five years earlier:

> He used to cry – I'll never forget it for as long as I live – as soon as I'd gone he was laughing happily, but it used to tear me apart. I used to pop back in the dinner hour to check.

A closer look at the ten recent starters would suggest rather more distress in the children than appeared from the whole sample. Four minders mentioned some distress which was confirmed by the mothers as usually a few tears and not lasting long; however one of the minders said it had gone on for some time ' . . . she screamed for an hour when her mum had gone.' In two cases the minders reported no trouble but the mothers felt that it could not have been easy:

> She said he was fine but I think he cried a bit – I didn't ask because I didn't want to know.

> She got a bit upset. (The minder had said ' . . . fine, she never asked for Mummy at all.')

One minder reported 'upset at first – quiet sobs' which the mother did not mention. The remaining three pairs gave a quite trouble-free picture.

Conversation and communication

We were interested in whether minders and mothers had the opportunity to talk to each other regularly about the child's progress, and whether they actually did so; also whether they were able to discuss and resolve problems which arose. We therefore asked about the previous day – or the most recent day the child went to the minder's – whether they had talked and what they had talked about. We also asked about any worries either had had in the last month about the child's eating, sleeping, toilet training, general behaviour or language, and whether they had discussed these between them.

Daily exchange of information

Most of the mothers either took or collected their child, or both, and so had the chance to talk to the minder. And most mothers seemed to feel that they had plenty of opportunity to talk about the child, and that more could be found should the need arise, although the minders did not seem so sure. Nearly two fifths of the minders felt they would like more opportunity to talk to mothers.

When we looked at whether mothers and minders had in fact talked to each other 'yesterday' it was less clear that the opportunities were being used to exchange routine information about the child on a daily basis. Ten mothers (16 per cent) had not seen the minder at all because they did not take or collect their children; in these situations it was usually the child's father who did, and we got the impression that fathers did not go into the house to the same extent as mothers. A further 24 mothers (38 per cent) had taken or fetched their children yesterday and had seen the minder, but they had not talked about the children: 17 had chatted about other things, and seven had not stopped to talk at all. Only 29 mothers (46 per cent) had chatted to the minder about their children either in the morning or, more often, in the afternoon when they were somewhat less rushed. It would seem, then, that on a day-to-day basis over half the mothers and minders did not feel it necessary to discuss their children's progress that day. Was this because all was going well, and they only talked about the child when things were wrong? We shall consider problems over the child next.

Worries and problems about the child

We wanted to know here what sorts of things worried minders and mothers, and whether they discussed them with each other. We should remember, though, that they were not necessarily confronted with the *same* problems, since children might behave differently at home and at the minders' – indeed, we shall see in a later chapter that many of them do. We should also bear in mind that people do not necessarily worry about the same sorts of things, so that what may be seen as a problem by one may be dismissed as a passing phase by another. We have not attempted to consider here the comparative severity of the problems minders and mothers raised as worries, but simply taken their own definitions.

On this basis, out of the 63 children where we interviewed both mother and minder, 46 were described either by the mother (in 33 cases) or the minder (in 28 cases) as causing at least one worry during the last month; in a third of these both minder and mother mentioned the same worry. So in less than a third of cases were the children giving *no* cause at all for concern, although sometimes the worries of the remainder *were* very slight. We will look in more detail at each of the problem areas.

Worries over sleep during the day

Seven minders and one mother spoke of worries about daytime sleeping or resting. These all turned out to be worries not about the child resisting being put down for a rest but about him being excessively sleepy and tired. The minders tended to blame the parents for this, in letting their children stay up too late, as these typical comments illustrate:

He goes to bed too late, so he's tired in the day.

He's always tired, he goes to bed too late; it's not fair on either of us.

She tends to keep him up very late to play . . . he gets tired.

The mothers sometimes saw things rather differently. As one mother put it:

> I think she sleeps too long there; I can always tell [when she's had a sleep] . . . I'd rather she went to bed early.

Another mother had asked the minder not to let her son sleep in the day, because if he did she was unable to settle him until about 11 o'clock at night; the minder, for her part, was worried because she could not keep him awake – he would fall asleep while playing, and in fact fell asleep during our interview. They were trying a compromise where he was put down for a proper sleep, but only for an hour. All together nearly a quarter of the mothers reported difficulty in settling their child at night.

Some of these worries about sleeping and resting may well reflect the difficulty of agreeing on a routine which suits both the minder and the working mother, who may either want to keep her child up a bit later if she does not see him during the day or who may be so tired after a day's work that she wants to get him to bed early. However it is also possible that the child's noticeable sleepiness at the minder's may be a sign of withdrawal, a form of escape from a situation in which he is unhappy. We shall see in later chapters that this may be so for some children.

Worries over mealtimes

Eating problems were more frequently reported than sleeping ones. Nine mothers and 12 minders mentioned a problem, usually about different children but in three instances about the same child. So there were 18 children all together, or just under a third of the sample, who were giving cause for concern. Twelve of them were described as having a poor appetite – including all three whose minder and mother both reported the same worry. Another child ate too much, and one had a temporary loss of appetite because of sickness and diarrhoea. In the remaining four cases it was not so much appetite as the behaviour associated with eating: slow or messy eating, or throwing food about.

Worries over toilet training

Eight children were described by either their mother or their minder as having some problem in this area, but on the whole they did not sound very severe. There were some complaints from minders that mothers were unwilling to start training as early as they themselves would have wished, but in general they seemed to cooperate with each other. Some mothers were very pleased with the way minders had managed to toilet train minded children along with their own, and one minder said that her own child had learnt more quickly from seeing the minded child. One or two of the problems did sound more serious, with relatively old children persistently wetting the floor and furniture in what was felt to be a deliberate and aggressive way.

Illness

In addition to problems of this kind, there was the question of actual illness. We asked whether the child had been ill in the last six months and, if so, how this had been coped with. In those cases (22 out of 28) where the illness had involved 'minding' days, 15 of the parents managed to take time off work. Of the rest, two children were in hospital and six went to the minders; two of these had colds, two were cutting teeth; one had influenza, and one had chicken pox – as had the minder's own children. So physical illness did not appear to be a major problem; the minders were not being asked to take responsibility for very sick children, to the possible risk of their own being affected, although they occasionally wondered if being minded when poorly was in a child's best interest. As one minder said, '. . . I did think he needed his mum that day . . .'.

Problems of behaviour and speech development

A rather different set of issues confronts us when we look at what minders and mothers defined as behaviour problems, or problems of language development. A fuller description of these problems and their relationship to other factors in the children's lives is given in a later chapter; we shall briefly summarize them here in order to complete the picture of what worried the mothers and minders.

Worrisome behaviour was reported of 30 children, almost half our sample. The sorts of things minders and mothers raised ranged from really rather disturbed, withdrawn or distressed behaviour to relatively minor problems such as having picked up bad language or annoying habits. Some were described as 'a stage he's going through', but others were thought to be longer term. Six children's problems, one in five of those whose behaviour was causing concern, were mentioned by both mother and minder. The majority, though, were mentioned by either minder or mother but not by both. The absence of comment from the other person may reflect failure to recognize or admit to a problem, a different view of what constitutes a problem, or simply the occurrence of the worrying behaviour in one setting only – as was certainly the case with some children.

What happens when problems do arise?

Having considered briefly the sorts of things which worried minders and mothers, we can now look at whether they discuss these worries with each other and manage to resolve the problems, and whether each is satisfied with the way the other is managing.

As we saw earlier, 46 children were reported as having a problem of some kind in the last month. One of these had only started at the minder's the day before, so there had been little chance to deal with the situation. Of the remaining 45, there had been some talk about the problem, or at least an attempt to raise it, in 37 instances. In 18 cases it seemed that the worries were discussed in such a way that progress was possible and everyone seemed pleased with the arrangements. One minder said:

> . . . anything and everything I talk to her about . . . she usually has a cup of coffee, she's never in a rush.

This mother was herself very pleased with the standard of care the minder was giving her child. Another pair gave no evidence of specific discussion of worries, but felt they had no problems in talking to each other and were happy with the arrangement.

In the remaining 25 cases, however, over a third of our sample, there was ample evidence that talking about problems was not easy, and although in ten of these cases the mothers seemed satisfied with the minder, the long-term prospects did not seem good. One minder, who had tried to talk to the mother about eating and toilet training, blamed her failure not on a lack of opportunity to talk but on the mother's 'unresponsiveness'. Another wanted to discuss a child's eating and sleeping, but said: 'I feel guilty waylaying her. . . . I'd like to sit down and have a good chat instead of trying to grab her here and there.' A third had tried unsuccessfully to discuss an eating problem, but she felt that further efforts 'wouldn't do any good; they'll still do what they want to do.' The parents said of the minder in this last case that 'she keeps us talking when we'd rather not. . . .'

Parents, for their part, tended to describe more specific issues which they hesitated to raise: here are two, not connected with the minders quoted above.

> Mrs Thomson and her children tend to swear rather a lot, but I don't feel I can mention it.

> I don't agree with her making Tom eat all his food, but the same goes for Lisa [the minder's own child] so I just try to avoid being there at mealtimes.

Perhaps the best way of illustrating the extent to which communication can be inhibited is to look at three arrangements viewed from both sides.

The first was a quite recent arrangement; it seemed as though minder and mother really knew very little about each other; the child was rather anxious and fearful according to the parents.

> MINDER: I'd like more opportunity to discuss [him] with her . . . she just flits in and out and it doesn't give me much time to talk to her.

> MOTHER: I think she was worried at first, I don't know whether she'd done it [minding] before. . . . I don't have a lot of time to talk to her as I'm in such a hurry and I think she's very shy.

The second was a quite longstanding arrangement between two women who both said that it had come about because of their friendship:

> MINDER: I don't think she likes me at all – she's just using me, she knows no-one else would put up with it. . . . I can't talk to her, we just argue.

> MOTHER: I've talked to her about giving Andrea too many sweets and biscuits, but it makes no difference . . . it's not worth a great battle, it's better to have a good relationship. She babies her, she thinks I treat her too grown up.

The third seems to reflect a complete misunderstanding of each other's intentions.

> MINDER: She's very difficult to talk to.

> MOTHER: I've no criticism of her . . . I wasn't expecting her to bring him on, she was simply somewhere to take him and look after him – not like a playschool.

We wondered whether minders and mothers who were already friends would find it easier to talk to each other over worries which arose, but this turned out not to be so. We have already cited one example where the minder felt the mother was exploiting their friendship. Another was a minder with a handicapped child, who was minding the daughter of a friend she knew quite well. She admitted that she felt a deep resentment towards her friend for, as she saw it, abandoning her healthy and delightful child for the sake of her career. She could not bring herself to talk to her friend about this, saying:

> When it comes to the point I don't say anything . . . I could have the opportunity if I wanted it, but I have conflicts in my own feelings. . . .

Altogether there seemed to be evidence that in 20 per cent of arrangements made between friends, this friendship between mother and minder did not make communication any easier; sometimes it impeded it, or was itself the cause of problems.

Communication viewed overall

Looking at communication overall, it would seem that where things are going relatively smoothly, with few anxieties, minder and mother have no communication difficulties: 30 per cent of the children were not causing any worrry, and in none of these cases did minder and mother have problems in talking to each other. When problems do arise with a child, however, communication becomes difficult in over half the cases, and is often withheld altogether, partly because the other person is seen as unreceptive, and partly because of a fear that talking will make matters worse for the child.

Both minders and mothers may well be being realistic about this. While it would be nice to think that a problem shared is a problem halved, there may be good reasons to think it will be doubled. Both are mothers, and for either to mention a problem may be seen as a criticism of the other's way of raising children, or as an admission of her own inadequacy. We shall see in a later chapter the extent to which minders define themselves as competent mothers: that is their main, often their only, qualification for looking after other people's children. We shall also encounter the pressures on mothers to be seen as no worse parents for having jobs. A child with a problem is a reflection on both of them, so even to bring up the problem may be both an implied aspersion and a threat to the continuance of the arrangement.

It is also possible to explain our findings the other way round: good communication may prevent problems arising for the child, while poor communication and mutual lack of respect between minder and mother may make for a tense and hostile situation which the child will sense and to which he will react.

Why do arrangements end?

We have no direct evidence from our random sample of children about what reasons terminate arrangements and with what relative frequency, but we have from a variety of sources some indirect information about particular groups of children and minders which may give us an idea of what leads to breakdown. For example, we asked the minders about the last three children they had minded who had now left; and we asked mothers whose children had been to other minders before their present one why they had changed minders. We also asked ex-minders why they had given up minding.

Looking first at the last three children our active minders had minded, we can see from Table 4.2 their reasons for going. The two most frequent reasons, accounting for nearly half the 122 children, were that the child had gone to primary school or that the family had moved away. In a further fifth of cases the child had left because his mother had stopped work, often to have another baby. However, there may have

	Number	Percentage
Child went to school	29	24
Child's family moved away	29	24
Minder asked mother to remove child	11	9
Mother removed child	13	11
Mother stopped working	24	20
Temporary arrangement	11	9
Other	4	4
Total	122	101

Table 4.2 *Reasons given by minders for previously minded children having left*

been others who stopped because of problems over the minding, as these two examples suggest:

His mother finished college and they moved – but I'm not sure that was the real reason; they were a very reserved family.

His mother gave up work but I wouldn't have him back – they [the parents] messed me about. . . .

The two groups which seem to suggest that arrangements were ended rather than came to a natural break are the 11 children whom the minder asked the mother to remove, and the 13 where the mother removed him without being asked. In the former the minder usually found the child's behaviour too difficult to cope with, either because he was very distressed and unhappy or because he was difficult and disruptive, and a bad influence on her own or other minded children.

The minders did not apparently know why the other 13 children had been removed by their parents. Sometimes this was done very abruptly; one mother telephoned on a Sunday afternoon to say her child would not be coming on the Monday or ever again – though he had been going to the minder for more than two years. It seems quite likely, although we cannot be sure, that the level of communication between minders and mothers was not very good even before the break in these cases; certainly it was not very good afterwards. On the other hand it is possible that these were cases where the minder had tried to discuss a problem with the mother who had taken offence.

Turning now to the children in our sample who had been to previous minders (15 children had been to 20 minders): their mothers gave a variety of reasons why their children left. In the majority of cases it seemed that the minder's situation had changed: her own children had started school, her family had moved or she, herself, had gone back to outside work. In only four cases did the mother remove the child because things were not right, in two because she was not satisfied with the minder and in another two because the child was unhappy.

Looking at why the 26 ex-minders had stopped minding, we find that very few gave reasons that were overtly to do with minding itself. The majority had either stopped when their own children went to school or when they had got a job – though the fact that they got a job may imply that they had had experiences of minding which had put them off. Indeed we saw in the last chapter that they were more likely than the active and inactive minders to mention things they disliked about minding. Among the dislikes, nine objected to being taken for granted by parents, and eight had a bad relationship with a child or parent, including disagreements over standards of care. While we do not have enough information to be sure, it looks as though many of these arrangements broke down because the minders, for one reason or another, stopped minding and went back to work rather than because the children had, for instance, gone on to school.

Since the active minders are more likely to be those who like minding and are committed to the children they mind, while the ex-minders and the childrens' previous minders are less enamoured and committed, the differences between them in the termination of arrangements are only to be expected. It is clear that sampling currently active minders will inevitably produce a more stable and harmonious picture of minding, than taking a random sample of children at the

outset of minding and following them through. Even so,
nearly a fifth (and probably more) of the past minding
arrangements with our active minders had broken down in
unhappy circumstances, and in nearly a third of current
arrangements mother or minder felt unable to talk to the
other about worries over the child. We shall also see in future
chapters that minders found it very distressing to look after
unhappy or difficult children, and several felt they would
have to stop looking after those children. We cannot say,
necessarily, that it was the failure to discuss problems which
was causing arrangements to break down; indeed, it seemed
that minders and mothers often preferred to avoid touchy
subjects in order to prolong the arrangement.

Are the arrangements well made?

In this chapter we have looked at how mothers and minders
get together, how they negotiate and agree on their relationship, how they start the child off, how they talk to each
other about progress and problems, and how they part
company. What seems to emerge overwhelmingly at every
turn is the haphazardness of the arrangement. Things are not
planned, they happen. There are no rules to follow in
conducting affairs: minders and mothers seem to stumble
into a rough and ready accord.

Underlying the whole process there appear to be all sorts
of assumptions about children and their needs, and about
mothering, and all sorts of ambiguities about who controls
the situation. Both mothers and minders seem to assume that
minders, as fellow mothers so to speak, can look after any
child, and that one child is much like another. Minders seem
to place little importance on the individual characteristics of
the child they are about to take on, and mothers seem as
little concerned to inform them. They may both also be
nervous and inhibited by the ambiguous nature of the
balance of power between them, with the mother 'owning'
the child and the minder owning the premises, and by a

general embarrassment over money and terms – made even more awkward if they are already friends.

When it comes to helping a child settle down at the minder's, by and large most mothers and minders show little concern or awareness of the problems, or if they do, are not able to establish a clear procedure. Some mothers do not even think it is necessary for the child to meet the minder at all before he starts, and some minders do not insist on it. In this respect minding is probably different from other forms of day care which do increasingly insist on mothers staying to settle their children.

Once the child has started, things seem remarkably trouble free. Very few minders report any marked difficulties in the first week. In view of the lack of concern over preparing the child, and the unceremonious way some children are just dumped, we find this surprising and also rather worrying. It may sound odd to be worried at the *lack* of difficulty, but we suggest that it would be more normal for children in this situation to protest vigorously. We shall see in a later chapter that minders frequently describe minded children as 'good', and many children are noticeably quiet.

Many arrangements continue on these trouble-free lines, with mothers and minders on very friendly terms and both satisfied with the other; if worries do arise they are not taken as too serious and are sorted out – or sometimes glossed over in the interests of preserving a friendly relationship. In a substantial minority of cases, however, the minder or mother wants to discuss a problem but does not feel the other would be receptive. This brings us back to the question of powers and rights. Mothers recognize that minders have the right to run their own homes as they wish, and that they cannot ask them to make exceptions for their children. Equally minders are very aware of mothers' rights to decide what they want for their children, and conscious that they tread on very sensitive ground if they think to question what they do. Sometimes things do indeed get fraught, and the arrangement breaks down, often at short notice and without explanation.

For the minders and children in our survey, arrangements had not reached this point, although a few seemed to be nearing it. In most cases though our mothers and minders were on very good terms and often considered themselves friends. This being so, we found it strange that they did not talk to each other more about the children, but rather chose to chat about other things. We have suggested some reasons why they may have preferred to avoid talking about children's problems and progress; and it is also true that in some cases there may simply have been insufficient time.

In the next two chapters we shall look in greater detail at the minders' and mothers' lives.

5

The life of a childminder

In this chapter we aim to trace the childminder's point of view: to set out the 'terms' of the job – hours, pay, conditions of work (at least as they were in Oxfordshire at the time of our survey) and also give an idea of how minders see their work. We can only be fair to minders, and make suggestions for changes in policy that are practical and workable, to the extent that we understand minding from the inside.

Conditions of work

This is rather a misleading title, since most of the minders we saw seemed not to conceive of their minding in such terms. They saw it as not so much a job with fixed hours and conditions, as a sideline, something they fitted into their main commitment, which was looking after their own families; something they enjoyed on the whole and which had the advantage of bringing in some extra money. But let us stick for the moment to the idea of a 'job', with conditions in the usual sense, since that makes it easier to describe what was involved.

Hours

These varied considerably: they ranged from under four hours a week to over 50. About two thirds minded full time and about one third part time – by which we mean under 30 hours a week. A few of the full-timers worked really very long hours (see table 5.1).

	Number of minders	Percentage of minders
0–9 ⎫ part-	5	8 ⎫
10–19 ⎬ time	12	18 ⎬ 37 part-time
20–29 ⎭	7	11 ⎭
30–39 ⎫ full-	8	12 ⎫
40–44 ⎬ time	29	44 ⎬ 62 full-time
50+ ⎭	4	6 ⎭
Unclassifiable	1	2
Total	66	101

Table 5.1 *Total hours per week spent minding*

Nearly two thirds were working a five-day week, but there was plenty of variation amongst the rest, all the way from one day a week to seven (verging almost on fostering). The vast majority (85 per cent) had the children the same days and times each week. But there was a small group that catered to the needs of parents with variable working hours, and *their* schedules changed from week to week. Sometimes the children stayed for the night.

So minding varies a great deal. At one extreme, it can involve looking after a child for three hours once a week and, at the other, it can cover five days a week and occasionally weekends too. Being flexible about hours, within reason, does not seem to bother the minders. (What does bother them is parents' not sticking to agreements made, arriving late to collect, not letting them know when they decide not to bring their children.)

Numbers of children minded

At the time of our survey, there were surprisingly few children to be found at each minder's. Over two thirds of the minders were minding only one child, and a quarter were minding two, not counting their own (see Table 5.2). Only two minders were minding more than three children, and

then no more than five *at any one time*. The one woman
minding eight did not have them all together.

	Number of minders	Percentage of minders
1	46	70
2	15	23
3	3	5
4	0	0
5	1	2
6	0	0
7	0	0
8	1	2
Total	66	102

Table 5.2 *Total numbers of children being minded*

Two-thirds said they currently had vacancies, in that
they were not minding their registered maximum number.
Neither did minders seem to be overwhelmed with inquiries
from parents. As many as half the registered minders in our
sample had no children to mind when we saw them, though
they still considered themselves minders. These were the
ones we called 'inactive'.

This picture could not be more different from the one we
have of inner-city minding, where parents must accept that
their children will be among many at the minders'. It is
interesting to speculate whether full employment for women
in Oxfordshire would create a similar situation there.

Money

Viewed as a wage, minders' pay was abysmally low. Their
gross rate per hour (in 1977) worked out at an average of 30p
an hour*, ranging between 11p and £1·50. The rate per child
was even lower: an average of 26p, with extremes at 8p and
75p.

Out of this minders had to pay for meals, snacks, bus fares,

* All averages quoted are means

sweets and ice creams, toys and play materials, wear and tear on their furniture, breakages, and anything else that might crop up. In some cases they even paid the children's play-group fees. Mothers often brought babies' food with them, but minders themselves almost always had to supply food for older children. In keeping with their overall attitudes to their 'job', most did not know exactly what their expenses were and found it difficult even to guess, but expenses there undoubtedly were. Eleven minders had insured themselves for their minding, so they also had an annual premium of around £5 to pay. There was only a small group of minders (one in ten) who were successfully claiming the refund, to which all registered minders are entitled, on the milk drunk by minded children. The vast majority either did not know of their entitlement, or found it all too much trouble.

On top of all this, minders had no guarantee of a regular income. This was not so much because parents did not pay on time (most of them did), but because when children did not come, whether because of sickness, holidays or just a parent's whim of the moment, by and large the minders did not get paid. A child might even be withdrawn altogether at a few days' notice.

However, the minders themselves did not see themselves as exploited. Almost two thirds said they were happy with their pay and only a fifth actually admitted they were not. They rarely mentioned money when asked directly what they disliked about minding, and did not even seem resentful at losing it through mothers' vagaries – they tended to resent only the personal inconvenience of being kept waiting. We gained the impression that many minders liked to feel that in a sense they were doing the mothers a kindness. They perhaps also felt there was no point in being unhappy when mothers could not afford more while their own pay was also low.

> We could all get on our soap boxes; for example I get £7·50 for working from 8.30 a.m. to 6.30 p.m. which works out at about 10p an hour. That's the sort of thing

people at work would go on strike for. But the mother is single, has to pay £19·00 per week for a one-bedroomed flat, and can only just manage the £7·50.

I couldn't ask for the London rate – because wages are that much lower.

But it is also true that some minders simply place a low value on their activity. Since they do not see themselves as doing a 'job', they do not expect a proper 'wage'. One minder felt it necessary to justify her 25p an hour: 'I feel I earn it'! Even when minders do put a higher value on their own work, it may be difficult for them to stick to their guns in the face of parents' attitudes. One minder made this point rather forcibly:

You have to be hard. A lot depends on the mother and father. It's quite an eye-opener – I had one father who thought I shouldn't be paid at all.

And yet we found signs that minders' attitudes might be changing; these were particularly noticeable when they came together in groups – for instance to discuss the BBC television series. Although those who attended may not necessarily have been typical of all minders, they did frequently raise the question of charges, and discussed money and the difficulties in setting new rates with more feeling than almost any other issue. The television programme that focused on money may itself have encouraged minders to expect a greater reward for their services. In the prevailing climate of opinion – that minders should put more into their work, try to provide more stimulating play opportunities for the children, and so on – minders will expect greater financial rewards and recognition to go with it.

Holidays

There were no fixed holidays for minders: none stopped minding during school holidays, except for two who did not mind during the summer and so preferred to take only teachers' children. But, when we asked whether minders had had a holiday of some sort during the previous year, it turned out that only 9 per cent had not. Most commonly they had arranged a holiday to suit themselves and their own families, and then informed the mothers in time for them either to take their own holidays at the same time or to make other temporary arrangements for looking after their children. It was clear that holidays were never discussed when minding arrangements were set up. This illustrates again the extent to which minding is unlike a job.

Physical conditions

Housing conditions seemed to us to be very good, particularly in comparison with inner-city minders on record. All the minders except one were living in houses as opposed to flats, and all but one had a garden in which the children could play. The vast majority also had a park or open land nearby which they could use. Seventy per cent had a telephone and 27 per cent had the use of a car on some or most days. All kept their houses well heated in winter, either just downstairs or overall, and only one reported severe damp. The type of housing varied from area to area – some people lived on pre-war council estates, some in private semi-detached houses of varying ages, often modern – but the common factor seemed to be physical conditions which were perfectly adequate, and often very good.

The children were allowed considerable freedom. Over a third of the minders said they placed no restriction at all on the rooms that the children were allowed in, and over half said either that they used all the downstairs parts of their houses for the children or that they excluded only their own bedrooms. Only one kept the child in a single room.

On the other hand, the fact that minders' homes were adult-centred territory – living rooms, for example, with televisions, three-piece suites and fragile ornaments –

obviously placed some kind of constraint on the children. Minders could not allow the kind of play that would have caused excessive wear or damage to their surroundings in the way that playgroup leaders or nursery school teachers might in a more child-centred environment. For example, they could not allow play that involved sand or messy things indoors (although some minders did allow water-play and painting in their kitchens) or indoor climbing or building activities. Only one minder had a room specially reserved for play.

Other commitments

Minders' own families were their first and major commitment. This meant that their lives already involved a good deal of shopping, cooking, washing-up, housework, attending to their own children's needs and taking and fetching them from different places. All these things they had to do whether they had minded children with them or not. In addition, the minders often had other regular commitments. Nearly a third were looking after at least one older child after school or in the school holidays or both. About a fifth also took in these children when they were not well enough to go to school, an example of the kind of flexible service that only minders seem to provide. A few of the minders also seemed to be providing continuous service to whole families: sometimes the older children were brothers and sisters of children currently being minded, or children who had come to be minded as under-fives. As far as the minders were concerned, however, this was just an extension of their everyday activities into a slightly older age group, and it involved them principally in fetching from school in the afternoons and in providing tea for more children.

Just over a quarter of our sample combined their minding, or had done in the past, with other part-time work, mainly cleaning. Whether they did this for extra money or for adult company, it must have meant that they were often tired and had little time to relax or be with their husbands. Almost another quarter had combined minding (or still were) with part-time playgroup work or playgroup courses, or both. Only two had done any full-time work since they had first taken up minding.

Family, friends and other minders

Husbands

We had expected husbands to be uninvolved in general, and to regard the minding wholly as their wives' province. However, a surprising number actually saw quite a lot of the minded children, played with them, and lent a hand in various ways. When we asked minders how their husbands felt about their minding, nearly two thirds made such comments as 'Oh, he doesn't mind,' and half that number said he positively liked it. Only 5 per cent of husbands apparently *dis*liked the minding. Three quarters of husbands helped out, and nine out of ten played with the children.

> He doesn't mind at all – he loves children. He talks to them and draws with them. He's normally busy in the garden and he takes them up the garden.

There was one particularly warm and involved husband:

> He takes them to the park, the shops, in the garden. He lets them help with washing the van – and at meal-times, especially when Anna first came and couldn't feed herself . . . She's a favourite and he is. She refers to him as Daddy. She won't go home without kissing him. She likes him here. . . . She likes a cuddle – she's a daddy's girl.

This one was unusual, but in general husbands did seem to be quite a strong source of support.

We looked for difficulties, mainly for strain in keeping children quiet when husbands were working on a night shift. But that was rare. More often husbands on nights seemed to take the most active part in the children's lives simply because they were around more in the daytime. One minder even regretted that her husband was no longer working at night:

> 'He used to help when he was on shift work. He would go in the garden with them; go to Newbury for the day – or Reading – in the car.'
> 'What do they do together?'
> 'Nothing now. They used to play when he was off shift.'

Minders' own children

This picture was less clear, and it is difficult to draw conclusions. When we asked what the rest of the family thought about their minding, about half said their children like it or loved it, or it was simply 'part of their lives' and by implication welcome. A further third said their children 'didn't mind'; only nine said there were mixed opinions in their families, with, for example, one child quite happy but another rather jealous at times. Just one minder said her child disliked it.

When we asked more specifically both whether there were any benefits for their children in having minded children there and whether there were problems, most said there were advantages, and they usually cited company, or the experience of learning to share. Not surprisingly it was most often the minders with under-fives who found company an advantage; learning to share seemed a more widespread benefit. A much smaller proportion – about two in five – were aware of problems in that their own children got less attention, or were jealous (unexpectedly, jealousy was not worse among the under fives). A very few felt that the minding restricted their older children in the holidays.

We felt there might well have been some reluctance among minders to mention problems for their own children to us, or possibly even to see them themselves. On the face of it jealousy, for instance, seems such a likely thing to encounter. But we have no more factual evidence either way, except that women who had given up minding did not give problems with their own children as a reason.

Friends

We had wondered whether minding might have cut down contact with friends during the daytime, as a result perhaps of the effort of taking out several small children at once, or a reluctance to inflict them on friends. But this hardly ever seemed to be the case. Two thirds said it had caused no change, and of the rest only half felt things had changed for the worse. The others apparently had few friends anyway (one 'wasn't the sort to mix much'). Several minders told us that they regularly took the children round to their mothers' houses for a cup of tea, or that their parents called on *them*.

Other minders

Most of our minders had at least a passing acquaintance with others in their area, but only a third of them had other minders as friends, and roughly the same number knew no minders at all. Only 18 per cent had met with other minders in a group during the previous month and even this is probably an unusually high percentage, due to the Social Services Department's meetings in connection with the BBC television series on minding (see Newton, Harris and Bryant, 1978) being broadcast at the time.

Contact with the social workers and others

Once a minder has registered, unless she happens to move house (in which case she has to go through the whole process of registration again), her contact with the Social Services Department seems minimal (See Table 5.3). Of our minders, only 42 per cent had been visited during the past three months. Twenty-one per cent had never been visited at all, even though some of them had been minding for as many as five years. At the time of our interviews, there may in fact have been a few more visits than usual, due to the efforts made by the three specialist workers to get minders to come to the television meetings. Many of the minders thought they had been visited for this reason, but the Department may have been intending to make these visits anyway so we cannot be sure of this.

Recency in months	Number of minders	Percentage of minders	
0–3	28	42	56
4–6	9	14	
7+	12	18	39
Never	14	21	
Don't know	3	5	
Total	66	100	

Table 5.3 *Recency of social services department visits*

We wondered whether any group of minders might have been receiving more visits than the rest, for example because they were seen as in need of advice or support by social workers. We looked to see whether those who had previously been minding illegally had been singled out as in any way needing more visits than the rest, but we found in fact they were getting about the same number. Most minders who recalled having been visited thought it had been just a general check up. How frequently they had been visited depended a little on where they lived, and the proportion who claimed they had never been visited since registration was roughly the same from area to area, ranging between 17 and 33 per cent, but these differences were not significant.

There were only two minders being paid directly by the Social Services Department for children referred by them, and no-one was having a low rate paid by a parent topped up by the Department. There were no grants of any kind available for safety equipment like fireguards, or play materials, or useful equipment like double pushchairs, although occasionally specialist workers were able to help individuals out informally if they had been given or loaned any equipment by members of the public. Recently it had become possible in a few areas for minders to take advantage of the cheaper bulk-buying rates offered to members of the Pre-School Playgroups Association on things like powder paints and plastic aprons.

Minders were visited even less often by health visitors than by Social Services officials. Health visitors have no particular statutory responsibility for minded children as such though they do have a responsibility for all under-fives. But fewer than one quarter of the minders could recall ever having been visited by a health visitor about a minded child.

However, most could name at least one official they could contact if problems arose, and about a third had in fact made such contact in the past – usually in connection with either the health or the behaviour of a minded child. On the whole, though, our minders did not seem either to be anticipating problems or to be particularly enthusiastic about contacting anyone.

We asked minders if they were happy about the service offered them by the Social Services and the health visitors. Questions like this in social surveys are known not to produce much dissatisfaction, so it is not surprising that 58 per cent said they were perfectly content. However, a fifth felt the service was either non-existent or irrelevant to them, and another 8 per cent said they were actually dissatisfied.

Even though most were quite happy, over half were able to suggest improvements: most commonly more contact with the specialist workers, and also help with equipment and toys, or meetings with other minders.

We asked minders whether they would prefer to be employed by the Social Services Department, putting the question in terms of being paid by them instead of by the parents. This was clearly a new idea to many minders, so perhaps not too much store should be set by their answers.

Forty-four per cent said no, 29 per cent yes, the rest were not sure. Of those who said no, some added that they might have answered differently if they had ever had problems with parents over money, but so far that had not arisen. One minder pointed out that if she was not paid by the parents she would have no way of getting them to bring the child more regularly by demanding payment for absent days.

Minders' feelings about their work

As we saw in Chapter 3, many of the minders had been minding for several years already: nearly a quarter for six years or more. Moreover, nearly a third said they wanted to carry on indefinitely. Of the other two thirds, most had no definite plans, but thought they might stop when their own children started school.

Likes mentioned	Percentage of minders* (N = 66)
Pleasure in children's company and affection	73
Feeling of doing worthwhile job/giving a service	18
Freedom/being their own boss	12
Earning their own money	9
Other including everything mentioned by fewer than 9 per cent	30

* Percentages total more than 100 since minders often mentioned more than one like.

Table 5.4 *What minders said they liked about minding*

What did they like or dislike about their 'job'? Almost all could find one thing they really enjoyed – most often the children's company. (See Table 5.4).

> I enjoy being with children – I'd like two, I think they'd be more company. I enjoy having him around. I treat him as one of my own rather than thinking I've got you till 4 o'clock then you go home.

> To have young children in the house. It's company. I like young children's company.

Next most frequent was the satisfaction of doing a worthwhile job and, third, company for their own children.

Just under half could suggest one or more thing they *disliked* about minding (Table 5.5).

Dislikes mentioned	Percentage of minders* (N = 66)
Getting taken for granted/put upon	17
Feeling tied or restricted	15
Tension over standards of care/discipline or wish to criticize how parents were bringing up a child	11
Problems for own children	6
Problems with parents over money	8
Other, including anything mentioned by less than 9 per cent	11

* Percentages total more than 100 since minders often mentioned more than one dislike.

Table 5.5 *What minders said they disliked about minding*

The commonest was 'getting taken for granted, put upon or used by parents'.

> I don't like being messed around. Like Friday. I had a busy day. I'd got everything ready for him and suddenly he's not coming. I'm a very busy person.

Almost as common was the feeling of being tied or restricted, but this must be widespread among any group of mothers at home with small children. Some mentioned tension with parents over standards of care or discipline and a few also mentioned money.

It seemed to us that the pleasures of minding centred round the children, and the dissatisfactions round the parents. In fact, for about a quarter of the minders, the difference between their feelings for the children and their feelings for the parents made their minding an upsetting and difficult experience at times. These were all minders who felt concern, or strong affection, or both, for a child they were looking after, and felt at the same time that the parents were rejecting him, neglecting him or mishandling him in some way. Minders in this situation often felt angry with the parents on the child's behalf, and not surprisingly had difficulty in knowing what or how much to say to them.

> I seem to end up with children whose mothers don't look after them properly. They ask me to do things and I can't refuse 'cos I'm afraid for the kids. They ask for food and money. . . . Children should be with their parents always. I've been very good to Kenny but it's still affected him. He's very insecure. He keeps asking if I love or like him all the time. It's going to be bad for him . . . she brings him in the morning half naked and soaking wet. . . . I could tell her to go to hell any time but I worry for Kenny. . . . I feel responsible for Kenny.

This minder, uniquely, was even thinking of giving minding up because of this sort of thing.

There was another – quite separate – quarter of our sample who felt very opposed to the idea of mothers of young children going out to work at all, though they almost always acknowledged it was necessary in exceptional cases. (As we saw in Chapter 3, altogether almost half of the total sample expressed some views of this kind.) They normally took the view that the children suffered, and they must have had mixed feelings about minding these children. It also seemed likely that they would disapprove of parents whom they felt had no special grounds for working, although only five said so. Typically, disapproval was expressed like this:

> I don't think it's fair to the children. No matter how good the minder, they still miss out on a bit of love, don't they?

> I wouldn't do it – only if I really had to money-wise. I never palmed mine off. . . . These I've had just get bored. Part-time is a bit different. But the others – well, I wouldn't do it.

Much more commonly, cross feelings were expressed about personal inconvenience, or (less often) about loss of fees, due to the unreliability of a few parents. These difficulties with parents were on the whole more than compensated for by the pleasure of caring for small children, so much so that at this point in our study we really felt very optimistic about child minding as a service in Oxfordshire.

How minders spent 'yesterday'

Asking this question has the great advantage that it concentrates on particular events, rather than on global ideas. We went through the day, step by step, recording what the minder and the child were doing and whom they were with, from the time the child arrived to the time he was collected. The 'diaries' that resulted give a very detailed picture. Here are two that are characteristic, except that the second minder was looking after a baby.

Mrs Chester
Mrs Chester is a mother of four who has taken an extra child into the family from 9.00 a.m. till 5.00 p.m. each day. She is nearly 40, lives in Banbury and is married to a foreman at a local factory. She worked in a factory herself before she was married and has lived in the area for many years. She has been looking after her minded child since the child was a baby, starting as a favour to her mother, who is still a friend. The child, Sharon, is now three, a bright self-assured little girl. She and the minder seem attached to each other. The minder has four children of her own. One has already left home and the others are 14, 12 and 11. She doesn't see herself as a minder, since this is a one-off arrangement between her and her friend.

This is how she described the previous day. At 9 o'clock Sharon arrived; Mrs Chester had a chat with Sharon's mother, and from then until noon, did her housework, ending by preparing the lunch. Sharon played around her for the first two hours, then went off to watch *Playschool* on the television and played by herself for half an hour. At noon Mr Chester came home for his lunch, as did the three older children, so Mrs Chester served food for two adults and four children as usual, and they all sat down to eat together. At the end of his lunch-hour, Mr Chester went back to work and the older three children went back to school, leaving Mrs Chester doing the washing-up. When she had finished this, at about 1.00 p.m., she took Sharon to the local playgroup, left her there and went off herself to keep an appointment at the clinic. She got back to playgroup in time to fetch Sharon at 3.30 p.m., walked home with her and set to work to prepare the tea. Her own children came in at 4.00 p.m., and all the children had tea together. She cleared up and got her husband's tea ready for 4.45 p.m. when he was due in. Meanwhile Sharon went out to play with two of the older children, went up the road to the shops with them and played around in the garden until her mother came for her at 5.00 p.m.

Mrs Ripley

Mrs Ripley has three children of her own; like Mrs Chester she is also minding one other, but unlike Mrs Chester she does see herself as a minder, has minded other children previously, and is planning to take on another child in a few months' time. At 28, she is roughly ten years younger than Mrs Chester, and her own children are correspondingly younger at seven, five and three years old. The child she is minding, Kate, is six months old, and has only been with her a short time.

She has lived in Oxford all her life but has only recently moved to her present council house. She was a sewing machinist before she married, and after having children took up cleaning part-time to supplement the family income and spend some time out of the house.

For the past three years she has been minding on-and-off and combining this with a part-time evening cleaning job in a local office. She wanted to stay at home for her own children and took up minding both because she needed the extra money and because she liked looking after children.

This is how she described her 'yesterday'. At 8.30 a.m. Kate arrived. She put her in a baby buggy and took her, together with her own three-year-old, to escort her two older children to school. She then took Kate and her own child round to her mother's for a cup of tea at about 9.00 a.m., as she does every day. After about half an hour she took her three-year-old to nursery school, and then took Kate and her baby buggy on the bus two miles into town to the weekly vegetable market. Home at about 11.00 a.m., she fed Kate, changed her and put her in her pram, all of which took about half an hour. She then took her to fetch her three-year-old, got back at 11.45 a.m. and started to put her shopping away and cook the dinner. Soon after 12.15 p.m. Kate went to sleep in her pram, and Mrs. Ripley and her own child had lunch together. She washed up and tidied up the home until 1.45 p.m. when Kate woke up and needed to be fed and changed again. From about 2.00 p.m. she 'sat down' and played with both children for an hour, with the baby first on her knee and later on the floor.

At 3.00 p.m. she got both the children ready to go out to fetch the elder two children from school, so Kate was put back in her pram where she went back to sleep for half an hour. By 3.45 p.m. Mrs Ripley was back with all four children. She sat Kate up in the pram in the living room, and the other children talked and played with her, while she got some tea ready. They ate their tea and at 4.00 p.m. Kate's mother arrived to collect her, at which point it was just time to start thinking about getting her husband's tea.

Common features of a full-time minding day

We were impressed when reading all these accounts of 'yesterday' by features which minding days often had in common. The pattern was roughly as follows:

The minders would receive their minded children round about 8.15 or 8.30 a.m. and get their own families up, breakfasted and off to school by about 8.45 a.m., accompanying them or (if they were older) just sending them off. They would then wash up the breakfast things and tidy up the house a bit.

At some point there would be a trip to the local shops, usually combined with taking a child to school or playgroup. (Often the main shopping was done once a week or once a month, with their husbands and without minded children.) If there was a child of the relevant age, this child would be taken to a playgroup and fetched a couple of hours later. On these excursions out of the house minders sometimes had as many as three under-fives to keep their eye on at the same time!

Around noon, the minder would be preparing, serving and clearing away lunch. Often their husbands and older children came home to lunch, so this could be quite a busy time. They would therefore often switch the television on at about this point for the programmes for very young viewers.

Throughout the day they had to fit in children's rests and, if they were minding babies, special routines for them too. Their own and minded babies were generally fed at different times from the rest of the families. When the children were having rests, minders tended to do those jobs, like ironing, that could involve danger for small children.

Then at about 3.30 p.m. there were usually older children to be collected again (which involved taking the younger ones out again). The children then sat in front of the television, or out in the garden, while tea was prepared for them.

At odd times during the day, usually when there were only under-fives about, the minders would fit in their housework. Rather more than half said they deferred at least some of it until after the children were gone, but most reckoned to fit in some. They were often 'helped' by small hands and rarely had the chance to do it quickly by themselves. They might also have to fit in preparing vegetables for a main evening meal, or giving the children tea and then preparing their husbands' teas.

Most minded children seemed to be collected round about 5.00 to 5.30 p.m.

This complete account leaves out 'minority' activities, such as social visits – some minders went round to their mothers' houses for cups of tea, or over to friends' houses with the children. An important minority activity, involving perhaps one third of the minders, was the care of extra children – mentioned before – often the minded children's siblings aged more than five but less than nine – who came for breakfast, or tea, or even (not always the same children in this case) came full time during school holidays. For this group of minders there was always a houseful of children and a complex of meals and to-ings and fro-ings to be organized.

Implications

With lots of children to be taken, fetched, catered for and ministered to – not to mention husbands – it is *impossible* to give each child a great deal of attention. And minded children in these large 'composite' families seem to spend much of their time playing with other children, and generally being a part of large family life. They probably do not *demand* much attention from their minders either, as there is so much going on. Within this frame-work, however, some minders gave their minded children more individual attention than others; this ranged from none at all to about two hours a day. That is to say, some minders actually sat down and played with the children, or read to them, for a short time in the course of a day, others did not. Just over half had been actively involved with the child on the previous day (our measure included any reports, however vague, of having played with the children, but excluded time spent together on meals, nappy changing and so on). Forty-two per cent had not. The age of the children may have something to do with it, as the difference between Mrs Chester and Mrs Ripley suggests. Under-threes probably need more personal attention than three-, four- and five-year-olds, who may be quite content playing together. They also need more attention to keep them out of danger. There were some minders – like one widow with no children of her own – who had lots of time (and the inclination) to spend exclusively with their minded children.

In many cases minders struck us, too, as extremely good managers considering the kind of schedules that many of them maintained, and the numbers they catered for. Their ability deserves recognition. At the same time, we wondered if they were not rather too busy: were the children getting enough attention? We return to this later, when the time comes to focus on the children.

What minders are trying to do

It seems to us very important to get some insight into what minders see themselves as doing, otherwise debate about minding as a form of care can hardly be fully informed, and any attempts from the outside to improve the lives of minded children are likely to fail.

The questions we asked included 'What sort of person makes a good minder, in your opinion?' and 'What sorts of things do you think you should know about?' We asked whether any special training was really necessary for their work, and whether there was anything they themselves would like to know more about.

As Table 5.6 shows, minders tended to put forward patience, love of small children, an even temper, and a relaxed attitude to mess, as necessary qualities.

	Number of minders	Percentage*
Patience	39	59
Enjoys, likes, loves children and their company	33	50
Not too houseproud, can stand a bit of mess	28	42
Even tempered, easy going/adaptable/happy nature	19	29
Prepared to play with, talk to children on their own level	12	18
Has children of her own	9	14
Understands children/aware of child's point of view	6	9
Energetic, fit, active, prepared to take on extra work	5	8
Imaginative, has ideas for doing things with children	4	6
Good hearted, considerate, kind	3	5
Motherly/loving mother	3	5
Got to do it for more than just money	3	5
Other (mentioned by only 1 or 2 minders)	15	23

* Percentages total more than 100 because most minders mentioned several qualities.

Table 5.6 *What sort of person makes a good minder?*

Someone with lots of patience and time. You've got to love and be able to cope with all sorts of children.

I think you must never promise them anything you can't fulfil, and be fair to them and tolerant.

Someone who doesn't mind having kids running around. It's no good if you want the house to look just so.

Not me, I don't think. You need a lot of patience. You need to be organized.

They suggest a view of minding as warm-hearted, accepting, relatively passive caretaking. Very few mentioned any outgoing qualities. Less than a fifth, for example, suggested a minder should be prepared to play with or 'talk to children on their own level', and only four minders suggested she should be imaginative or have ideas for doing things with children.

Turning to the sorts of things they thought a minder should know about, we found that top of the list came first aid, which was put forward by half the minders. Second came commonsense or experience, or the knowledge of children you get from bringing up your own, which were suggested by one third, followed by knowing things 'about children's play', suggested by 29 per cent. We had noticed when listening to minders talking together in groups that safety and first aid concerned and interested them. Obviously they saw keeping their charges physically intact as an important part of their role! Furthermore, when we asked each minder in the survey whether there was anything she herself would like to know more about, the only item mentioned by more than five was first aid, suggested by eight. Knowing about children's feelings or about problems (such as illnesses or special needs) appeared very low down in the list, and were suggested by only 20 per cent and 6 per cent respectively. Two thirds of the minders could not think of anything they personally would like to know more about.

	Number of minders	Percentage*
First aid/accidents	32	49
Commonsense/have had own children	23	35
Children's play	19	29
Children/looking after children (unspecified)	16	24
Children's health, hygiene, nutrition, diet	15	23
About the individual child being minded	14	21
Children's feelings	13	20
Problems	4	6
Other (mentioned by three minders or less)	8	12

* Percentages total more than 100 because some minders mentioned several items.

Table 5.7 *What sort of knowledge should a minder have?*

These answers also suggest that minders regard their minding as a kind of motherly caretaking, with an emphasis on physical care. However, there was a substantial minority to whom children's play was important.

When we asked specifically whether minders needed to be given special training for their work, only 15 per cent gave a clear and unqualified 'yes', although an even smaller group (8 per cent) gave a clear, unqualified 'no'. The largest single group (45 per cent) was generally or partially in favour of the idea of training but held many different views on what it should consist of, whether they themselves would like to have some or whether they thought it should be for other, substandard, minders.

> It could be an advantage. My attitude altered when I did a playgroup course.

> Yes in some cases I know some people who keep the children in bed too much. The children seem quiet and slow to talk.

> Some probably need it, not me.

One third felt that only those without children of their own had any need for training.

> No. They get that from bringing up their own.

> In some circumstances, but if you've had children of your own that's better.

Most minders clearly felt that looking after minded children was much like looking after one's own.

In sum, it seems that minders see themselves as more than babysitters but less than professionals. They aim to act as motherly caretakers, using the valuable experience and commonsense they have gained from bringing up their own children, and treating their minded children just as they treat their own. Preschool provision was until recently categorized as care and education; most minders would put themselves firmly on the 'care' side. Only one mentioned preparing a child for school as part of her task, and very few acknowledged the importance of giving a child new experiences or stimulation, or of filling needs that were unmet in the child's home – for example, for stability, for a father, or for playmates. We came across only one who clearly saw herself as a professional. She had a residential childcare qualification, and was acting like a nursery schoolteacher to three three-year-olds, preparing them to read, deliberately allowing them messy play, and so on.

A substantial minority (but still fewer than one third) saw the value of play in children's learning. Whether the importance of play is gaining recognition particularly among childminders (perhaps influenced by the Social Services Department) or more generally among the population at large, we do not know.

We are also not sure how to assess minders' strong interest in first aid and the prevention of accidents. Of course, *all* mothers see children's physical safety as of paramount importance, but we were struck by the fact that minders did not take it for granted but brought it up as a matter for conscious concern. They did so, perhaps, not only because of their sense of responsibility towards other people's children, but also perhaps because safety was the one visible yardstick by which they could be judged. A mother can see cut knees or burnt fingers, but will not know if her child has had, for example, a nutritious meal, interesting things to play with and talk about, or generous attention from his minder, unless the minder actually tells her.

On this note we will leave the minders' viewpoint and turn next to the parents themselves.

6

The working mother's perspective

What was it like to be the mother of a minded child? What did an ordinary working day actually consist of? How did the mothers feel about having their children looked after by childminders?

We interviewed 63 mothers or main caretakers of the children (4 of whom were actually fathers*). These were the parents of the children we selected for special study. Although the interviews were shorter than those with the minders they were still quite detailed, usually taking at least an hour and sometimes much longer. As part of the interview, we asked parents as well to recount what they actually did all day 'yesterday' or on the most recent working day.

We divided our account this time into the following sections: first, the conditions of mothers' daily lives (jobs, hours, pay, ability to take time off when the children were ill, daily travel, housing conditions, what their children were like at home, and any help they received from outside agencies); secondly, how they felt about their work; thirdly, how they felt about the care their children were getting, and about the minders; fourthly, how they spent 'yesterday'.

Conditions of life

Altogether 54 of the mothers (86 per cent) went out to work, 8 per cent were students and 6 per cent (four mothers) were at home. These last four were employing minders either, for instance, to keep their children in contact with playmates dating from when they had worked, or else to gain part-time

* As before, we refer to all these caretakers as 'mothers', except where this obviously would not make sense.

relief from disturbed relationships. Leaving those who were not working aside for the moment, we will turn to the lives of the majority.

Jobs and hours

Nearly two thirds of the working or student mothers were working full-time, by which we mean 30 hours or more per week. (See Table 6.1).

	Number of mothers	Percentage of mothers	
40+	25	42	62 per cent full time
30–39	12	20	
20–29	11	19	36 per cent part time
10–19	6	10	
Less than 10	4	7	
Don't know	1	2	
Total	59*	100	

* We obviously did not include in this table the four mothers who were not working, but we did include the five students.

Table 6.1 *Hours worked per week*

Their jobs ranged widely in type. Two were doctors, two home helps or cleaners, eight were teachers, four nurses (including one health visitor), and four administrators of various kinds. There were two telephone saleswomen and two catering managers, one in training. The largest single group was of clerks, typists and secretaries.

Pay

Their net pay was on average much higher than the minders', and much more variable, ranging from under £10 per week net for the bottom 11 per cent to £40 or more for the top third.

Of the full-timers, roughly half (17 out of 35) were earning a minimum of £40 per week after all deductions. This contrasts markedly with the full-time minders, of whom about half earned less than £10 *gross!* Only four full-time minders earned over £20 and none earned as much as £40. These figures suggest that some mothers may be able to pay their minders considerably more than they do at present.

However the other 18 mothers working full time were on incomes of less than £40 per week net, and four of them on less than £30. Two of these four were students, one a casual fruit-picker and the other a telephone saleswoman – a single parent. The lone parents must have been very hard pressed financially and they probably had difficulty paying even the low rates they were charged.

The earnings of the part-timers told a similar tale. A third (seven out of 21) were earning a minimum of £30 per week net, and three of these were earning £40 or more. These highly paid part-timers seemed to be a relatively privileged group in the sense that none were single parents and all were in professional or semi-professional occupations like teaching or medicine. There were no part-time minders earning anywhere near these rates; almost all of them were earning less than £10 per week gross.

But there were plenty of mothers working part-time whose lot one would not envy. Half earned less than £20. Two of these were single parents, one a barmaid living on her own with two under-fives, and one an administrative clerk living with one child in her parents' home.

Time off work

We asked mothers how easy it was for them to take time off work if their children were ill, and how easy it was for their husbands. We also asked whether they lost any earnings or holidays if they did so. The vast majority felt it was fairly easy to take time off themselves, but only about a third did not lose as a result. It seemed that it was less easy for fathers to take time off, but on the other hand fewer fathers than mothers were likely to lose earnings.

Few of the mothers felt that their children's being ill was a problem – although not all had had to face it. This may have been due as much to the fact that minders will often look after moderately ill children (or mothers hope that they will) as to their employers' tolerance. About half of the minders had looked after children when they had colds or stomach upsets and occasionally even when they had infectious illnesses. Only a quarter had been asked but had refused. Some mothers remarked that their children came first and they were prepared to give up their jobs if necessary. One mother told us

> I just do it and if they don't like it they can have their job. I told them when I started that my family came first.

But she had not yet had to put this to the test. There were also a few who thought it best to hide the reason if they had to take time off work. 'I couldn't tell them she was ill but I can get time off,' said one mother, but she had sent her child to the minder as usual the last time she was ill, with a 'very bad cold'.

Daily travel

Some three quarters of the mothers had to take their children to the minders, and sometimes older children to school, before work and fetch them afterwards. Occasionally they went together with their husbands in a car, but fewer than half the fathers were involved in this way. Very few fathers did the taking and fetching themselves. However, we found no obvious evidence that travel and transport were a burden. Nearly three quarters of the mothers travelled by car, about one fifth walked and only two mothers used buses. Journeys on the whole seemed fairly short, and certainly the daily travelling was not something mothers spontaneously complained about when asked about the disadvantages of working.

The fact that so many went by car also means that these mothers were less likely to feel limited by distance in their choice of minder. This was another reason, then, why it seemed odd that they exercised their choice so little.

Housing conditions

The mothers' housing conditions were very similar to those of the minders. About two thirds had a telephone, most had a garden and only nine suffered from any damp. Over half kept their entire houses heated in winter. On the whole then, conditions seemed rather good.

However there was a small group for whom housing conditions were not quite so good, and these were the single-parent families. There were ten lone mothers and three lone fathers in this group, and for them there was significantly less heat, fewer gardens, and less comfort overall for themselves or their children. We did not ask about overcrowding, but several of the single parents had moved in with their own parents and were clearly very cramped – sleeping on sofas, and so on. It is difficult to make generalizations based on such a small group, but our findings certainly confirm the widespread concern felt about one-parent families and the added difficulties they have to contend with.

The children at home

We asked what each child was like in the mornings before his mother went to work, what he was like when she first got home, how his bedtime went, how long it took to settle him and whether he usually slept all night. We were looking for evidence of both good and bad times.

Three quarters of the mothers said their children were good-tempered or happy on the whole before work, only 10 per cent that they were really bad tempered or miserable then. A quarter said that they were tired or sleepy after work, and two fifths that they were hungry or thirsty. About a third said they were 'the same as usual' or 'no trouble', 'fine' or 'OK'; a fifth said they were affectionate or 'pleased to see me'. Nearly a quarter said something that indicated they were demanding – 'generally tired and a bit niggly and clamouring for a drink', or 'a bit overwhelming for a while'.

> She just requires a lot of my attention. Very demanding and very bossy – '*Get* me a drink' rather than asking properly.

> She wants to claw at you, grab at you for about ten minutes. She's quite irritable, telling tales, wanting a drink.

There was some evidence of enjoyment in about half the bedtimes, and nearly three quarters sounded child-centred. Here is one reply, chosen at random, to the questions 'What about his bedtime – is that usually enjoyable for either of you?' and 'What usually happens then?'

> Oh yes. He doesn't mind going to bed. If he gets tired before his time he'll say he wants to go to bed. It's the same every night. I read to him and we play.

On the other hand, there was evidence of bedtime problems for one in ten and, as we saw earlier, difficulty was reported over either settling or sleeping through the night for almost a quarter.

> I've spoilt him really. I have to stay there till he goes to sleep. He used to cry when I came down and it was easier to sit with him than come down and listen to him crying.
> [This mother's child took 20 minutes to go to sleep if she sat with him.]

I would think about three nights a week she'll wake some time during the night and come in to me, then she usually stays with me for the rest of the night.

We have already discussed the extent of problems and difficulties reported by the mothers; in general, whatever the nature of the problems, mothers did not seem upset or weighed down by them, or unduly worried about their children's behaviour or progress.

Support from outside agencies

There was very little evidence of any help or support from either health visitors or social workers. Twenty-seven of the 67 mothers had, as far as they remembered, *never* been visited by a health visitor about their child, and only 17 – just over one quarter – had been visited within the last six months. Three quarters of the mothers had never had any contact with a social worker about the minding of their child. One would not expect much contact with the Social Services Department, particularly since most specialist workers do not see contact with mothers as part of their brief, but the low coverage by health visitors seemed surprising. Perhaps mothers had been at work when health visitors had called, but only one mother mentioned having found a calling card pushed through her door. Only four of the unvisited 27 mothers had taken their children to the clinic in the last six months, so it cannot be that the health visitors were aware of them and saw no need to call. Nor does it seem that, at least for the majority, health visitors were seeing these children at their minders. Only ten out of the 27 had been seen at the minder's, and at least three of these had only been seen incidentally because the health visitor was visiting the minder's own child. So it looks as though these children were not receiving regular health checks, and this in a county relatively well endowed with health visitors.

How mothers felt about their work

Most mothers said they liked their present jobs and two-fifths found only good things to say about them, despite our probing for both likes and dislikes. Only one in five appeared unhappy with her work (see Table 6.2). Most mothers felt

Feelings	Number	Percentage
Likes job, gives only positive information	23	39
Likes job, has some dislikes	27	46
Dislikes, but some positive	7	12
Dislikes, nothing positive	1	2
Didn't know, no information	1	2
Total	59*	101

* We excluded the four mothers who were not working but left in the five students.

Table 6.2 *Feelings about present job*

there were advantages apart from the money attached to working, usually that they enjoyed it and liked the company

	Number* (N = 59)	Percentage†
I enjoy work	23	39
I enjoy the company of other adults	24	41
I like to feel a bit independent	5	8
Keeps me in touch with profession	10	17
Helps my child to adapt	2	3
Other children to play with	2	3
Improves my relationship with child	8	14
Better than Social Security	4	7
Prevents loneliness and depression	17	29
Other	18	31

* The four mothers not working are excluded.
† The percentages total more than 100 because mothers often volunteered several advantages.

Table 6.3 *Advantages of working*

of other adults. About a quarter were keeping in touch with a profession, and about a quarter more were consciously avoiding loneliness and depression (see Table 6.3).

> I've always liked going out to work. I don't like the boredom of being home all day – even with a child you still get bored.

> Mainly being able to talk to other people. I need other people.

> I have to live in a tiny flat with my parents – It gives us all a break. It's an interest outside the baby – especially at first. I knew no-one when I came. I made friends. It was my first life-line outside the flat. Contact with other people mainly.

Most mothers also felt there were disadvantages attached to working, despite liking their actual jobs. The dominant drawbacks were that it made life rushed and tiring and pushed housework onto evenings and weekends (see Table 6.4).

	Number*	Percentage†
Don't see enough of/see less of children and husbands	20	34
Life rushed and tiring/have to do housework evenings and weekends	28	47
Ill-effects on child, e.g. more demanding	5	8
Other	20	34

* The four mothers not working are excluded.
† The percentages total more than 100 because mothers often volunteered several disadvantages.

Table 6.4 *Disadvantages of working*

> [It's a problem] fitting in the housework, but it bothers me less now – I'm prepared to let things go a little bit.

> I'm always moving about – I've never got any time. Not enough time for the house and the children.

Seventeen felt they did not see enough of their husbands and children. For example

> Not being with Nancy. That's the only disadvantage. I pick her up and I don't know why she's in whatever mood she is in because I wasn't there in the day.

> [I mind] not being able to do all the things I'd like to do with the baby – for instance, I'd take her to gym classes.

But only nine mentioned any ill effects on the children.

On the whole, then, the majority of the mothers seem to be fairly happy with their working lot, admitting there is a price to be paid but willing to pay it. There is cause for concern, however, over a minority (about 12 per cent) who are *not* happy with working and who may prefer to stay at home and look after their young children themselves. Many of these are single parents, and it seems certain that some form of income supplement would enormously improve their – and their children's – lives.

How mothers felt about their children being minded

Every single one of the mothers said their children were happy at the minders', and most felt their children gained something from going there – the chance to play with other children, or to learn to play with them (see Table 6.5).

> Just the company of another child:

> She sees more children during the day including her sister's, as they go home to lunch there; so she [the minder] has six children to lunch.

About two fifths suggested 'learning to be away from parents' as a gain. The mother of a child minded part-time said:

> My opinion is I think it does children good to go away from you. It gives them independence. I wouldn't have it on an every day basis.

	Number* (N = 63)	Percentage
Learns to get on with other children/ has company	32	51
Learns to be away from parents	14	22
Gets individual attention	7	11
Meets other adults	8	13
More/different activities from home	5	8
Gains a substitute mother/father/ granny/family	5	8
Has another loving relationship (with minder)	3	5
Learns to share	3	5
Other	20	32

* Some mothers mentioned more than one gain.

Table 6.5 *What mothers thought their children gained from going to the minders*

Other 'gains' mentioned by more than a few were 'getting individual attention' and 'meeting other adults'.

We asked each mother, too, whether she felt her child was attached to his minder. About half thought their child *was* attached in the sense that he *liked* the minder or had a kind of 'aunty' relationship with her: 'Yes, [to child] you like Barbara, don't you?'. But only about a third thought he was very attached, in the sense of loving her: 'Oh yes – he's ever so fond of her, and her mother.'

The vast majority of mothers seemed to feel quite happy about the degree of attachment their child showed, and only one indicated real worry or negative feelings. It was interesting, though, that over a fifth made the point that they did not want their children to get *too* attached. There seemed to be some ambivalence: on the one hand, they wanted their children to be happy and knew that some degree of attachment to the minder would be necessary for that; but, on the other hand, the idea of their children getting too attached to others was, not surprisingly, quite threatening.

It *would* worry me if Ellen [the minder] got too attached to her. She's suggested Lisa goes as a weekly boarder when they go to their new house, which worries me a bit. It would be like having her fostered out.

I don't mind at all. There's got to be a certain amount of attachment or it just wouldn't work.

I would just have to accept it [if he did get attached]. She's a sort of granny figure. I wouldn't mind for four mornings – he's not likely to transfer all his feelings from me when he's so part-time.

That's fine with me. I'd rather it was that way.

As a measure of mothers' overall satisfaction with their present minder, we asked how they felt about the care she gave the child generally and in particular about the way she managed his sleeping, eating and toilet training. The replies are summarized in Table 6.6.

	Number	Percentage
Very good/very pleased	42	67
Alright/no complaints/OK	14	22
Good but reservations	5	8
Not very good	2	3
Total	63	100

Table 6.6 *Feelings about the minder's care of their child*

We also asked about mothers' relationships with their minders, and grouped their answers in Table 6.7. About half said they saw their minders as friends

	Number	Percentage
Was already a friend	14	22
Has become a friend	18	29
We're friendly but not friends	25	40
Mainly a business relationship	3	5
Too soon to say	3	5
Total	63	101

Table 6.7 *Mothers' description of their relationships with their minders*

She's a personal friend. She was before Peter went to her.

> She's becoming a friend. I didn't know her at all,
> gradually got to know her more. The sort of person you
> might invite in for a drink. Not like a cleaner who you
> just pay and that's it.

Another two fifths felt they had an easy relationship but no
more

> She's very easy to talk to about Sharon. She tells me
> little things that happen. If there are problems we
> discuss them. We have no contact other than that. . . .
> We only have Sharon in common.

Half the mothers felt they could talk to their minders
about their own personal life and problems, and half did not.
Of those who did some rather emphasized the mutuality of
the exchange, and in only one case was there evidence that a
mother regarded her minder as a strong source of personal
support, as we had expected young and otherwise unsup-
ported mothers might do. Characteristically, we were given
answers on the following lines

> Yes, we were brought up together anyway.

or

> No, I never do. Personal things, no. She doesn't and I
> don't.

> No. I wouldn't consider it. I wouldn't ask her advice
> but I might tell her what was going on. For example, she
> knows about Mum's illness.

All but three of those who saw their minders as friends also
said they saw them as someone to talk to.

It is difficult to relate what we found to what is known
nationally about satisfaction with minders' care. In the
national survey quoted earlier, Margaret Bone classified 71
per cent of mothers as 'satisfied', 14 per cent as 'unsatisfied'
and 15 per cent as giving no answer – a picture not dissimilar
to ours. On the other hand, our picture of broadly contented
mothers contrasts markedly with the results of research in
urban areas. Mayall and Petrie's (1977) London mothers

sounded much less satisfied than ours, although strictly speaking we cannot be sure as the measures were not comparable. They write,

> Nearly half the mothers wanted a complete change from the minder for their child. Dissatisfied mothers talked in terms of inadequate care (poor food, few toys, poor quality and quantity of attention by the minder) several argued that the minding situation is too private – you do not know what goes on there and you have no redress – or felt that the minder favoured her own child and neglected the minded one.

In the light of this, why were our mothers apparently so satisfied? It does not seem likely that they felt uniquely inhibited about offering criticisms, so the difference must be real. But whether it is due to better quality minding in this rural and small town area, or to other factors like good physical conditions and the small number of minded children we cannot yet say.

Despite their (usual) enjoyment of their work and their satisfaction with the care their minders were giving the children, many mothers still did not feel quite free of worry about their children. Two fifths made remarks that indicated to us that they felt slightly uneasy or guilty about having their child looked after by someone else, or were not altogether sure their child was happy. And with half of these there was quite clear evidence of some such doubts:

> I always feel a bit on the defensive about it. People always say, 'What happens to Billy?' and I say he's at a childminder and they say 'Oh' – and I feel very defensive.

> I miss the kids and I don't particularly like other people looking after them . . . , I've never left the children under any other circumstances. I've never been the sort of person who liked leaving them.

> The main thing is love she's not getting by me being at work – which is the only thing I worry about.

The others were more ambiguous, or referred to worries in the past only. One mother said

> I felt so guilty about dumping the baby on the floor and leaving her. I came out feeling dreadful. She didn't worry two hoots.

And another, asked if she thought her child was happy at the minder's

> I think you can tell. A child can't be really miserable without (your) knowing about it.

Was there any real basis for the unease of these *particular* mothers? The evidence suggests not. Their children's behaviour was no more likely to have worried either them or the minder in the last month than that of other children. Nor were the uneasy mothers any more likely than others to have reservations about the minder's care of their child.

It seems likely, then, that these mothers were experiencing some conflict whose origins lay either within their own feelings and attitudes or those of people around them, or both. They wanted to work, on the whole, but either did not want to leave their children with someone else or did not feel they *ought* to. This is no surprise in a society such as ours, which still maintains that mothers ought to stay at home and look after their own young children. We also saw in Chapter 3 that many mothers did not give 'minder' as first choice of care for their child and would have preferred something else, so they may have felt some guilt at having 'settled for second best'. Since we did not ask directly about unease or guilt, they may well exist beyond the two fifths of our sample who mentioned them spontaneously.

How the mothers spent 'yesterday'

Just as with the minders, we asked each mother to recount to us what she actually had done on the previous day (or the most recent working day).

Mothers' days showed more variety than minders'. They varied according to whether the mothers worked part- or full-time, whether they were single or married (and in the case of the latter what kind of division of labour or role-sharing existed with their husbands), whether their jobs (or courses) involved work at home in the evenings, and whether they were, for example, professional or manual workers. But, in one very important sense they were of course all similar, in that they were attempting to operate in two worlds at the same time.

The best way to convey both the variety and similarity is perhaps to let a number of accounts speak for themselves. Take, for example, the part-time computer programmer/researcher of 33. She got up at 7.00 a.m., got dressed, had breakfast with her husband and two children of four and seven, put the dishes in the dishwasher and cleared up and tidied up with her husband. At 8.30 she loaded the car up with her work gear and tennis things and left a quarter of an hour later with her own children and two others, to take them to school, and then on to the minder's. At 9.15 she left the minder and went to work in the car with her husband. She then did her day's work, fitting in a quick game of tennis. At 3.45 p.m. she collected her four-year-old, had a cup of tea with the minder, and went home by 4.30 to prepare the supper. Supper was eaten by all the family at 5.15 and she then took her seven-year-old to a swimming lesson, not returning home till 7.30 when she got both children ready for bed. From 8.30 till bed at 11.00 p.m. she watched television and chatted to her husband. This, then, was a full and busy day which included time for physical exercise as well as a special after-school activity for one child, *and* time to relax in the evening.

Contrast this with the young mother of 19, just married, who worked full-time as a clerk and had one child, a baby of eleven months. Her 'yesterday' was a Monday, and she had got up at 6.15 a.m., had a bath, washed her hair, dried it, got dressed, had a ham sandwich, got her husband a cup of tea in bed, dusted and washed up from the night before. At

7.30 she left the house for work, leaving her husband to get the baby up and the minder to collect him. She arrived at work an hour later at 8.30 a.m. and finished at 5.00 p.m. The journey home took an hour again, so she arrived at the minder at 6.00, stayed ten minutes, and then walked home with the baby. Once home she got his tea, bathed him and put him to bed, and then at 7.15 started to cook supper. At 8.30 she and her husband had supper together. At 9.00 she washed up, did some washing and sewing and went to bed at 10.00. This day didn't seem to have any space in it for recreation, and it sounded very tiring. This mother did not like her job either – she said it was boring. And her time with the baby sounded not only minimal but joyless. She said he was usually grizzly when she brought him home, so she liked to get him fed and out of the way as soon as possible.

There were also differences between the lives of the lone and the married mothers. The lone mothers had no help with looking after their children, or with cooking, shopping, housework, or taking and fetching their children, all of which had to be done alongside (in seven out of ten cases) a full-time job, and often in rather worse housing conditions than those of the married people. Most single mothers seemed to lead extremely tiring, hardworking lives – like the divorced mother of four children, aged nine, eight, seven and three, who worked full-time as a cook and had no car, or the divorced mother of two under-fives who worked full-time as a teacher, and had to mark homework at night as well as put the children to bed, do the washing and ironing, and so on. Nevertheless, according to their own perceptions they were coping, and they often gave the impression of having worked out efficient and well-organized routines or systems for doing so. In the case of the mother of four, for example, the older children just had to look after themselves a good deal – there was no other way she could have managed – and the nine-year-old had to take the three-year-old to the minder's each morning. In this way she managed to get enough time for them to relax together – the previous day they had watched television together for a couple of hours after supper – and she had had some time to herself to sit and chat with a friend for an hour.

The lone mothers differed in how they fitted all they had to into a day. Some, for example, did housework and prepared the evening meal before they got the children up in the morning, and some did it all at night. About a half gave the children extra attention, sometimes keeping them up in the evening. The other half seemed to give them minimal attention, or at any rate had not been actively involved with them at all the previous day. Not surprisingly, fewer lone mothers than mothers as a whole had managed to fit in some time with their children on the previous day. Some – like the teacher with her marking to do – had not managed to fit in any time with a friend or indeed any relaxation at all.

The lone fathers in particular should be mentioned. Two of them, on the break-up of their marriages, had gone to live with their parents, and one was living alone and very depressed in a council house. This last led a sad life. He worked full-time as well as looking after his three children of eight, six and four. He had been on his own for about six months, and was going about things very conscientiously but inefficiently: the house was very dirty when we interviewed him. From 6.15 a.m. he spent an hour in bed drinking cups of tea and listening to the radio before he started getting the children up. Then he got their clothes ready, washed, shaved, took the dog out and cleaned the children's shoes. At 8.30 they all left the house and he walked with the older children to school and the youngest to the minder. He walked back to the minder in the evening to collect his child and as soon as he got home spent an hour doing the washing by hand (despite a launderette within walking distance) and getting the tea. Then he went to the shop, changed the sheets on the beds, watched television for an hour with the children, put them to bed at 9.30 p.m., and went straight to bed himself. His whole life seemed to be consumed by just keeping going. He felt he did not have time to do even that properly.

A younger lone father was getting some help from his own

mother. He was in his late twenties, worked full-time in a power station, and had been living in his parents' front room since the break-up of his marriage. He was just recovering from what he called a 'virtual breakdown' and was obviously still a troubled man. His mother helped in the care of his four-year-old child, getting him up and taking him to the minder, collecting him and bathing him. She would also be in to baby sit when he went out after his son was asleep, so he was able to have some social life. Like the third lone father, who also had some help, he had managed to spend some time playing with his child 'yesterday'.

Looked at as a group, all the lone parents seemed to have very tiring and demanding lives. Sometimes their emotional lives were in some kind of transitional or difficult state too. One man was separated from his wife but still courting her.

Turning to the married mothers, we get the same sense of busy, tiring lives, especially in the case of those working full-time. But there was one big difference, and that was the fact that the husbands often did up to a half share with the children (and in one case slightly more than half). Although we did not ask directly about how much part the husband took, it emerged from all the accounts of 'yesterday' that they very rarely took part in the cooking or housework – it was a rare exception, for example, when a husband got breakfast – but they sometimes made the children's tea and quite often either took them or fetched them from the minder's, and helped with bedtimes. More than half of the fathers had played with their children or otherwise been actively involved with them the previous day. They read to them or played with them in the living room while their wives cooked the supper. One or two took them out to the park.

The husband of one of the full-time teachers was unusually participating. While his wife played with their toddler in bed, from about 7.00 a.m., he got up and brought them tea and juice. At 7.30 the mother got up, and dressed herself and the child, and prepared the lunch for their teenage daughter. At 8.15 she got to school, and the toddler was dropped off at the minder's to have his breakfast. After school she went at 4.45

p.m. with her husband to collect him, and they both chatted to the minder for a while, arriving home at 5.30. She got the toddler's tea, relaxed and changed, warmed a bath, put the washing in the washing machine, made the bed and tidied up, all while her husband played with him and got him ready for bed. At 7.45 she read a story to him and put him to bed. At 8.00 she had a sherry and a chat with her husband and they watched television. After half an hour she went off to cook supper, which they had on a tray at 9.00. At 10.00 she did some decorating for a Jubilee event and some general tidying up, until 12.30 when she went to bed.

However, at the other end of the scale, there were also a few husbands who had little to do either with the children or with running the home.

Some married mothers got up very early (for example at 6.00 a.m.) to do the housework, others did not get up till 8.00 or so. They usually had time to themselves from about 8.30 p.m. onwards, which they most often spent watching television and chatting with their spouses. More of the married mothers were involved with other activities and organizations. For example, some had time to do gardening, decorate rooms together, be active in parent-teacher associations and so on, where, not surprisingly, there had been no sign of any of these things with the single parents (except for one father who was working on his new house). Some did their housework at night when their husbands were out. Nearly two-thirds had had time to play with or otherwise give some attention to their child on the previous day. On average, each married mother spent three and a half hours with her child on the previous day, although not necessarily actively involved with him all this time.

There was no evidence of widespread strain, or of a feeling of not being able to cope with everything that had to be done, amongst the married mothers, although there were one or two who *were* finding it difficult. One woman with three children had embarked on an intensive secretarial course involving homework as well as attendance at college all day: her husband was helping a lot but they were both finding it a strain. In contrast were one or two phenomenally energetic young couples who fitted a tremendous amount into their lives and seemed to thrive on it. There was a catering manager of 24, for example, with two children under three, whose day started at 6.45 a.m. and ended at midnight. In between she fitted in a full day's work, looking after the children, a trip to the supermarket, cooking three chickens for her work the next day, housework, and an excursion out for a drink with friends. However she had not had time to play with her children the previous day, or in fact to do more than dress, feed and ferry them.

This illustrates some of the ways in which their lives as a group differed from those of the minders. Most striking was the fact that they were much more involved with the outside world – the world, that is, outside children, playgroups, schools and home – and in this sense their lives and horizons were less restricted. At the same time they had a price to pay, if only in terms of the sheer physical work to be done. Some did their housework when the children were around, others did not, as we saw with the minders. Some made time to give their children some special attention, others did not, again just like the minders. Interestingly mothers working full-time gave their children no less attention than mothers working part-time; if anything, they were slightly *more* likely to have played with their children the previous day, although the difference was not significant.

On the whole, the mothers were gaining a great deal from the part the minders were playing in their lives. Most could enjoy their jobs in the knowledge that their children would be cared for during whatever hours were necessary, and they duly expressed great satisfaction. Generally, there did not seem to be great stress in terms of housing conditions, hours, low pay, travel, or ability to take time off work if the children were ill – and here minders were providing an extra service in that they were often willing to take mildly sick children. What was more, minders were looking after their children at rates they could afford – in a few cases, we felt, well below what they could have afforded.

Single parents had particular cause to be grateful to child-minders, in that they usually were obliged to work and they could not have afforded crèches or private nursery places, even if any such had been available. The conditions of their lives often seemed very hard, and we were struck by the fact that minders often seemed the only outside support available to them, in circumstances where they needed much more.

Some mothers were nevertheless slightly uneasy or doubt-ful about whether they were doing the right thing by leaving their children. This can be explained in part by the fact that society at large disapproves of them. The official view, at both central and local government level, is that life would be much more straightforward if mothers of young children would stay at home and look after them. This attitude is reflected in the low priority given to providing care for their children. We can also see how many minders echo these views in their criticism of, and hostility towards, the working mothers whose young children they mind. The climate of opinion is as yet little affected by the world wide trend of married women to continue working, or by the women's movement, or even by changes in the law, which, for instance, now protects women's jobs when they have babies. So it is small wonder that mothers who do decide to work feel that they are doing something mildly or even seriously reprehensible.

In spite of their unease, and in spite of the number of mothers having recent worries about some aspect of their child's behaviour, *all* of them told us that they thought their child was happy at the minder's. We wondered whether some mothers felt a need to defend themselves against the painful knowledge that their children were not in fact happy, parti-cularly when they were not in a position to do anything about it – as many were not.

On the other hand, some other mothers faced an equally unpleasant suspicion that their children were *too* happy at the minder's, and that they themselves might lose their unique place in his affections! So despite the positive role of minders, we were aware of inherent difficulties.

We have already seen in Chapter 4 the extent to which mothers, and not just those mothers who have to work and consequently have to put their child out to minders, seem to feel quite powerless to make changes. Having found a minder who seems good and who is willing to take her child, settled a few basic details like hours and pay, and having seen the arrangement under way, the mother has no say over, or even much knowledge of, how the minder actually looks after her child. In a way she has given her power and control to the minder for the time her child is with her. She might make a few requests, for instance that her child has a sleep, or not, but even these will not necessarily be granted. There is usually an unspoken assumption that the child fits into the minder's family routine and rules, and does not get special treatment. Indeed this assumption was not always unspoken —some minders make it clear that they aim to treat the minded children like their own. If a mother finds herself in disagreement but does not want to rock the boat, her best course of action is probably to try to avoid knowing about what upsets her, or witnessing it.

It is worth emphasizing all this, since it does appear to be one of the most fundamental issues. How different it is from the kind of arrangement whereby a mother employs some-one to look after her child in her own home. At home a mother has by definition provided her own evironment, in the form of toys and play materials, a standard of cleanliness, food and so on. And on her own territory she is the employer, so she is in a stronger position to dictate the arrangements, particularly if she makes it clear from the start what she wants. A mother/minder relationship, in contrast, is not that of employer/employee, whatever else it is.

All these forces and human reactions are likely to affect the way a child experiences his life at home and at the minder's. It is high time now to shift our focus on to the child himself, which we do in the next two chapters.

7

The minded child: Life at the minder's

In this chapter and the next we have the children's viewpoint. First, in this chapter, we shall concentrate on the practical issues: how old are the children; how much time do they spend at the minder's; what do they do there; where are they taken; whom do they meet? In the next chapter we will look particularly at the relationships between minder and child, at the child's behaviour, and at whether he seems to be thriving.

The children and their present minding arrangements

How old?

The great majority of the children in our sample were at least a year old and a third were aged four to five years (see Table 7.1). The oldest had just had her fifth birthday and was about to go to school; the youngest was a baby of five months – the only one under six months old.

	Children selected for special study (N = 66) Percentage	Children not selected for special study (N = 32) Percentage	Total (N = 98) Percentage
Under 6 months	1·5	0	1·0
6–11 months	6·1	9·7	7·2
1 year to 1 year 11 months	21·2	9·7	17·5
2 years to 2 years 11 months	22·7	12·9	19·6
3 years to 3 years 11 months	13·6	32·3	19·6
4 years and over	34·8	35·5	35·1
	100	100	100

Table 7.1 *The ages of the minded children*

It is clear, then, that at the time of our survey very few mothers in Oxfordshire were having young babies looked after by minders, although it would seem that a few years ago it was more common for them to do so. Taking the age at which the children in our study had started with their present minder, 22 per cent had been under six months old, and a further 9 per cent between six and eleven months. (Since these figures are only for starting with the *present* minder, the actual proportions who had started as babies under a year old would probably be even higher.) One reason why there had been a diminution in the number of babies being minded by the time of our survey may have been that the preceding year was a time of recession and high unemployment: married women with young children may have had difficulty finding work.

The large proportion of children aged between four and five years indicated that the minders in our sample were about to 'lose' one third of their minded children to the primary schools. We have talked elsewhere of the shortage of children to mind, particularly in some areas of the county, and this four-year-old 'bulge' will make them even scarcer, at least in the short run.

Present arrangements

The children spent vastly different amounts of time at the minders', from as little as four hours on one day a week to as much as 70 hours spread over seven days a week (See Table 7.2). The mean number of hours per week was 30·2: about half the children spent more than 30 hours a week at the minder, and over a third more than 40 hours; about half went each working day, Monday to Friday, and two children went at weekends as well. The time they spent at the minders' was not related to their age; younger children under three years old were just as likely to go for more than 30 hours as the older ones.

Hours	Children selected for special study (N = 66) Percentage	Children not selected for special study (N = 32) Percentage	Total (N = 98) Percentage
Less than 9	13·6	12·9	13·4
10–19	19·7	19·4	19·6
20–29	15·2	12·9	14·4
30–39	10·6	22·6	14·4
40–49	36·4	25·8	33·0
50+	3·0	6·5	4·1
Unclassifiable	1·5	0	1·0
Total	100	100	100

Table 7.2 *Number of hours children were minded per week.*

For at least half the children, then, being at the minder's accounted for a sizeable chunk of their waking lives, at least as much as full-time nursery school, often considerably more, and without normal school holidays. For these children, life at the minder's may become a relatively more important influence on development (and home life relatively less important) than it will for children who are minded for short periods on odd days.

By and large the arrangements were constant for each child each week, but a fifth of the children did not go regularly on fixed days for fixed hours. This was usually because their mothers' working hours varied, but sometimes because their mothers failed to take them. The child with the most unpredictable schedule was an eighteen-month-old boy whose parents both did some night shift work. He might go during the day for some of the time, overnight at other times, and sometimes not go at all for a while. At the time of our visit he had not been to the minder for three weeks, but the previous day had been left there for a long stay of three days and two nights. It seems likely that such unpredictability would increase a child's anxieties in general, as would – for such a young child – so long a period of separation from his parents.

The majority of the older children (71 per cent of the three- and four-year-olds) went to playgroups and nursery schools or classes as well as going to their minders, and this was equally true whether they were minded full- or part-time. Usually these were half-day playgroups, but three children went to nursery school, two for half days and one full-time. One child combined being looked after by a relative in the mornings and a minder in the afternoons.

Sometimes the arrangements were even more complicated. In particular one girl, Karen, aged four and a half, went two mornings a week to a private nursery school and went to one minder for those two afternoons plus one other full day; for two other full days she went to a different minder. Her mother liked this arrangement because if one minder was ill she could fall back on the other. At the time of the interview this arrangement had been in force for two years (during which time one of the minders had given up to have a baby and had been replaced by another) with no obvious ill effects. Neither Karen's mother nor the one minder we interviewed had any problems with her. She seemed very alert, sociable and happy, and her language was very advanced.

The playgroup arrangements were sometimes suggested and set up by the minders themselves, particularly if their own children were already going. And sometimes it was the minder, not the child's mother, who took him there on his first day. The advantages of a playgroup for the child – presumably the opportunities for play and for playing with other children – seemed taken for granted, and no-one suggested any disadvantages. Yet it is possible that having to cope with two or more new environments outside the home could make already insecure children even more anxious.

How long had present arrangement lasted?

Table 7.3 shows how long the children had been with their present minders, not just the 66 children we selected for inclusion in our study but for all the children attending the sampled minders. Nearly two fifths had been going for at least a year, and one fifth for at least two years. A few children had been with the same minder virtually from birth until starting primary school.

	Children selected for special study (N = 66) Percentage	Children not selected for special study* (N = 25) Percentage	Total (N = 91) Percentage
Less than 1 month	15·2	8·0	13·2
1–5 months	18·2	20·0	18·7
6–11 months	24·2	44·0	29·7
12–23 months	18·2	16·0	17·6
24 months and over	24·2	12·0	20·9
Total	100	100	100

* Excluding 7 children for whom there was no information.

Table 7.3 *Length of present minding arrangement*

Not surprisingly the length of the present arrangement was related to the age of the child, the older ones being those who had been there longest. It is reasonable to suppose that some of the arrangements for the younger children would in their turn become long-lasting ones. Since 28 per cent of the minders were planning to mind indefinitely and a further 17 per cent intended to carry on until their present minded children went to school, it would seem that a substantial minority of the children were with minders who accepted the responsibility for providing continuity of care and seeing them through their pre-school years.

On the other hand nearly a third of the minders said they intended to give up minding and go back to outside work when their own youngest child started school. Eight of these minders were looking after minded children who were younger than their own youngest child and who would presumably have to move to another minder, and one or two had already asked the mother to find someone else. These eight minders made up one quarter of those with preschool children of their own.

Previous caretakers?

For nearly half the 66 children in our sample the present minder was their first experience of being cared for by someone other than their mother. Of the 34 children who had been elsewhere first, the great majority had been to only one previous caretaker, and only five children (8 per cent) had been to more than one. We can compare this to Mayall and Petrie's London minded children, 28 per cent of whom had been to *three* or more previous minders. There was, therefore, little evidence in Oxfordshire to support the idea that minded children in general suffer repeated moves from caretaker to caretaker.

The 34 children had between them had 43 previous caretakers. By far the most common was another minder (47 per cent of previous placements), and the next most common was a relative (19 per cent). Day nurseries and crèches accounted for 11 per cent each, playgroups for 8 per cent and nursery schools for only 3 per cent.

Fifteen children had been to a previous minder, some of them to more than one, so between them they had been to a total of 20 minders. About half these arrangements had ended because of changes in the minder's situation, for example because the minder went back to outside work (4), moved house (2), had a baby (2), became ill or fed-up (2) or because her own child started school (1). In the remaining cases the reasons were mainly due either to the child's family moving away (3) or to the mother removing the child (4) – in two instances because she found the minder unreliable, and in another two because the child was distressed. As was also found in the London study, the duration of these previous arrangements was mostly rather short, between two and six months, although two lasted 12 months.

The five children who had been moved about most are of interest because they illustrate the chance events to which minded children can be subjected. Three of these children had had two previous moves before their present minder, one had had three and one as many as five previous moves.

Nine of their previous caretakers had been registered child-minders, three had been unregistered neighbours or friends, and two were full-time nursery places.

The child with the most moves was a girl, Molly, aged nearly four when we saw her. Both her parents worked for a government department, and her mother had returned to work when Molly was three months old. Molly spent the next three months being left with a neighbour, but her mother found this arrangement unreliable so she left her with a friend. This lasted six months until the friend gave it up because her husband found it inconvenient. Molly then spent eleven months with a registered minder until her parents moved. She then spent fourteen months with another minder, when her mother crashed her car and had no transport to take her there. She then went to a third minder who left the area six months later. At the time we saw her she had been with her present, and fourth, minder for three months.

Another child, Frank, was a year old when his mother became a full-time student on a social work course. He had been to two previous minders, both of whom had given up minding and taken on outside jobs within three months of having him. At the time of interview he had been with his present minder for seven months, and was nearly two years old.

Stability

How stable, then, were these present arrangements with minders? It would seem that a substantial minority were rather more stable than other studies have found, both in the length of time they had already lasted and their likely continuance. With five exceptions we found no evidence that children had been moved repeatedly from caretaker to caretaker.

We must qualify this picture, however, on two counts. In the first place it should not be too readily assumed that long-lasting arrangements are necessarily good ones, as we shall see in the next chapter. In the second place our method of taking a sample of minders at one point in time, the day of our first visit, increased the likelihood of our picking up the long-lasting arrangements and missing the short ones. By extension we were also more likely to pick up the more committed and locally well-rooted minders. Although the children's histories of previous care showed that a quarter had changed minders, usually because the minder could not continue to look after them or had taken an outside job, only one of these previous minders came up in our sample. We also found that most of these arrangements with previous minders had been very short lived.

By contrast it will be remembered that when we looked at the last three children who had left the minders in our sample (see Chapter 4), we found that these arrangements had lasted longer and had more often come to a 'natural' break, for example when the child went to school. We also found approximately one arrangement in ten which ended when the minder asked the mother to remove her child because of his distressed or disturbed behaviour. We shall see in the next chapter that a few of the arrangements for our sample of children were about to break down for similar reasons. While it is understandable that minders may prefer not to keep such children, they may be just the children who most need a stable and understanding caretaker.

Life at the minder's

Playspace

We have already seen in Chapter 5 that the minders' houses were generally of a high standard, and that all but one had gardens. Our interviews usually took place in the main living area, which was where the children normally played in-doors. This was often a through dining-and-sitting room and so quite large, and we rated two thirds as being spacious and comfortable with plenty of room to play. Moreover only one child was restricted to this one room, while one third were allowed free run of the house and a fifth were allowed everywhere except the minder's own bedroom. Another third were not allowed upstairs but could go anywhere downstairs. The children were also generally allowed free access to the garden, and some spent the interview moving between the garden and the living room; 62 per cent had spent some time in the garden on the previous day.

However, as we also saw in Chapter 5, not all these living rooms, even though spacious, were very suitable for small children. Some of them had very good quality furniture, or stereos, and ornaments from which the children would have to be kept away, and some were extremely tidy and carefully kept. These were usually minders whose own families had grown up somewhat. Also in about a third of the sample we felt the main play area was small and cramped and rather uncomfortable for the children. So not all of them, by any means, enjoyed spacious and suitable premises.

Toys

What did the children have to play with when they got to the minders'? Because other writers have found a relative dearth of toys for minded children we asked to be shown *all* toys even if they were upstairs.

Recall that we noted the presence or absence of toys in eight categories (1) books; (2) soft toys; (3) toys for imaginative play; (4) construction toys; (5) small manipulative and shape exploring toys (such as posting boxes or jigsaws); (6) noisy toys; (7) paper, pencils, paints, scissors, playdoh, and so on; (8) 'physical' equipment, such as riding or climbing toys, and outside equipment such as swings, sandpits, and climbing frames. We also rated them, using three-point scales, on their quality, condition, variety, age-appropriateness, and accessibility, and on whether they were sorted and usable or all jumbled up.

Three quarters of the minders were providing toys in six or more of the eight categories, and nearly half had at least one toy in all eight categories. Moreover, between a half and two thirds had scores of three on many of the ratings, which meant they were providing a lot of toys in very good condition which were easily available for the children to help themselves, were appropriate for their age and well sorted.

At the other extreme eight of our minders had toys in three categories or less, and between a quarter and a third were rated as providing a few toys of limited variety, in a poor condition, often out of the children's reach or jumbled up, and not suitable for the ages of the minded children. A few of the minders explicitly stated they they did not believe in toys as the children preferred to play with kitchen equipment such as plastic bowls and wooden spoons.

When we looked at the toys in the children's own homes we found a similar picture: about the same proportions of parents as minders were providing either a good or a poor selection of toys. From the individual child's point of view, taking his particular minder and home, the children with a very good supply of toys at home generally also had a very good supply at the minder's – and about half the children were in this situation. The only aspect on which home and minder differed significantly was the age-appropriateness of the toys. The child was more likely to have age appropriate toys at home, not surprisingly since his own toys would be bought for him while at the minder's he would normally be using toys belonging to the minder's children.

There were a small group of children who had very good toys at home and very poor toys at the minder's, and another small group who had much better toys at the minder's than at home. Six children had very poor toys in both situations.

We can say, then, that minders were by and large providing as good a collection of toys as the children's parents were, and that the standard of toys was reasonable or good. On the other hand between a quarter and a third had poor toys at their minders', and one in eight did not have even a minimum range of toys to play with there. Since the great majority of the children were over a year old, this cannot be very satisfactory – and the fact that their toys were just as likely to be limited at home does not in itself ameliorate this. Mayall and Petrie also found about a third of London minders providing poor toys.

Given the appallingly low level of minders' pay, it is not surprising that some do not spend money on buying toys for other people's children. Yet it may not be just a question of money. If we think back to the minders' aims discussed in Chapter 5, we remember that most minders did not place any great emphasis on providing stimulating play opportunities for minded children; nor did the mothers in Chapter 6 seem to expect them to do so.

Playmates

Do minded children usually have other under fives to play with? Two thirds of the children in our sample did, either the minder's own or other minded children, or both. They often spent long periods with these other children. For example, on the previous day half of them had spent more than four hours in each other's company, and nearly a third more than $5\frac{1}{2}$ hours. It was clear from what minders said and from watching the children play together that some had formed very close friendships, and especially with minders' own children of a similar age. We noticed, albeit not systematically, that these friendships tended to follow a certain pattern in which the minder's child was the leader and the minded child very much the follower. We shall return to this point in the next chapter when we look at the behaviour of minded children.

The minded children often had slightly older children to play with after school or in the school holidays, since half the minders had a child in primary school and a number looked after other children of this age. On the other hand one third of our sample of children were in the position of being the only minded child with a minder who had no preschool children of her own – and the majority of these (15 out of 23) had no primary school age children either. Of these 23 children, 11 were minded full-time and 12 part-time. However ten of them, including four full-timers, went to play-groups some mornings so could play with children there.

There was, then, a substantial minority, 13 or one fifth of our sample, who would not normally have other under-fives to play with at the minders and who did not go to play-groups.* All but three of them were over a year old, seven were full-time and three of the full-timers were over three years old. These children may have been able to play sometimes with visiting children, and we know from the time budgets that minders did have friends and relatives with children who dropped in for coffee and so on, but this was not usually on a regular basis.

We can note here that the picture found in London was quite different. There it was very rare for a minded child to be the only preschool child: 38 per cent were with three or more and 16 per cent with five or more other under-fives (Mayall and Petrie, 1977).

The child's day

On the day preceding our interview (or the most recent day the child had gone to the minder's) three quarters of the children had spent six or more hours at the minder's, and half eight or more hours – at least as long as a day at primary school and often considerably longer. What were they doing while they were there? Where did they go? Whom did they see? To find some answers we looked again at the diaries of 'yesterday' which formed the basis for the minders' days in Chapter 5, but this time from the point of view of the child. We obtained diaries for 64 of the 66 children.

It was very striking reading through these diaries how the

---

* Our method of sampling children probably resulted in an over-representation of these children.

children's days were governed by the minders' personal and domestic routines, and how relatively few minders set aside time to do things with them. For most of the children their day was spent either in playing about in the house or garden while the minder did her housework and cooking, or chatted to her friends, or in ferrying the minder's children to and from school, doing her shopping or laundry, and visiting her neighbours and relatives. About three quarters of the children's days were like this, the main variations on this basic theme arising from whether the child stayed near the minder or played largely in another room or the garden, and whether he was on his own or with other children. We give some examples, randomly chosen, below.

One group of children, about 15, tended to play largely with another child in the living room or garden while the minder got on with things elsewhere. An example was Rosie, aged nearly five, whose day lasted $9\frac{1}{4}$ hours:

> Rosie arrived at 8.45 a.m., about the time the minder's children left for school. For the first half of the morning she was out in the street riding her bicycle with the minder's daughter of the same age and a friend of the daughter's. The minder was indoors making the beds and preparing the lunch. The children came in and watched *Playschool*. They then went to the shops with the minder for half an hour, and collected her children from school for lunch. After lunch they all played outside while the minder cleared up, then they went back to the school, and on to visit a friend of the minder's and her baby. The adults chatted to each other indoors while Rosie and the minder's child played in the friend's garden. On the way back they picked up the other children from school. The children all watched television in the living room while the minder prepared the evening meal in the kitchen. Rosie was collected by her mother at 6 p.m.

A second group of about ten children tended to play on their own, often in the garden. An example of this group was

Rachel, aged four and a half, who spent 9½ hours at the minder's:

> Rachel arrived with her brother at 7.30 a.m. They both played with bricks in the living room, the minder cleaning and tidying upstairs, until the brother went to school at 8.45. Rachel went on playing alone for another half an hour, and then went and played alone in the garden for two hours while the minder did the washing-up and the washing. For the last part of this time she was joined in the garden by the minder's married daughter and her baby. After lunch they were all in the garden for an hour, the adults talking and Rachel playing round about. Then the daughter left and the minder went in to do the dishes. Rachel stayed alone in the garden for another hour and a quarter until her brother came back from school. Both children then played in the garden while the minder prepared the evening meal in the kitchen. They were collected at 5 p.m.

A third group of about nine children spent most of their time in the orbit of the minder, following her about, 'helping' with housework, while she tended to stay in the same room as the child. This group seemed on average slightly younger than the first two. An example was Terry, aged 23 months, who spent eight hours at the minder's

> Terry arrived at 9 a.m. and started playing with the minder's own son of two. For the first part of the morning both the boys went around with the minder wherever she went, into the kitchen to tidy up and upstairs to make the beds. Then they watched *Playschool* with the minder in the same room. They all stayed in the living room, the children playing around the minder. A friend and her two children came for lunch. After lunch they all stayed in the living room while the minder fed her eleven-month-old baby. Then the children all went into the garden while the adults did the washing-up and chatted. The children were in and

out, and eventually everyone went into the garden. Then the friend left, and Terry and the minder's son watched the children's television with the minder in the same room. Terry was collected at 5 p.m.

The fourth group of about ten children had in common a very high rate of coming and going with the minder which barely gave them turn-around time to do things in the house. An example for this group was Rupert, aged two and a half, who spent an eight hour day there.

Rupert was left at the minder's with his baby brother at 9 a.m. He played with the minder's son, Peter, aged four, while the minder got ready to go out. Then they walked to the playgroup to drop Peter off, and walked on to the shops. They got back at 11.15, and Rupert played by himself for half an hour while the minder put her shopping away and prepared lunch. At noon they went out again to fetch Peter from the playgroup. They then had lunch, after which Rupert had a sleep for an hour from 1 to 2 p.m. When he got up he played around for about an hour with Peter, mostly in the same room as the minder. At 3 they went out to fetch the minder's three older children from school, and got home an hour later. Rupert then played with all the other children for about an hour till his mother fetched him at 5 p.m.

These groupings are only rough ones, and sometimes they overlapped, for example if the child spent most of the morning on his own and most of the afternoon with another child, but between them they illustrate what seemed to us to be the main features of their day. None of these diaries revealed much detail of *how* the children were actually playing or what they were playing with. This may have been partly because we did not insist on enough detail when we filled them in, but the minders often gave considerable detail about other aspects of the day, such as the times and places of their various activities.

Only 19 minders (30 per cent of our sample) mentioned specific play activities they had carried on with the children 'yesterday', such as painting, reading books, playing with plasticine, or cutting out. We exclude vague reports of 'playing together' or time spent on meals or nappy changing – although we include one minder who described nappy changing as a time for having a tickle and a romp together on the floor. Often minders found time to do several different things together, and we counted 39 different activities betweeen the 19 children. Thirteen children had had stories read to them, often for quite long periods, eight had done painting, colouring and drawing, three had done cutting out, and five had done messy things such as playing with water, dough and plasticine. Other activities included lego, jigsaws and tiddlywinks, and physical games such as cricket, kite flying, dancing and so on. The atmosphere of these days came over in colourful little details that seemed to us to set these 19 minders quite apart from the others, and we quote two randomly chosen examples.

> Gillian was nearly four and spent $10\frac{1}{2}$ hours at the minder's. She arrived at 7.10 and played with another minded girl in the conservatory (an area leading off the kitchen), with the minder in and out getting the breakfast and getting her baby son dressed. After breakfast they all played in the conservatory with pastry. At 10.30 they moved to the garden and played with water siphons and containers. At 11 they had a milk shake and a biscuit. The minder then played with paper and pencils with them in the conservatory till *Rainbow* came on the television – about butterflies. After the programme they went back to cutting out, crayoning and writing with the minder. After lunch the minder mowed the lawn while the children played with the wheelbarrow and some bricks around her. From 2–3 p.m. the two girls had a rest, the minder settling them with a ten-minute story. During their rest the minder washed up, got the evening meal ready, had a coffee and wrote a letter. When they got up she put records on and they all danced together. They then got more toys out of the cupboard.

At 4 p.m. they watched *Playschool* and had tea. After that they read some more stories. Gillian was fetched at 5.20.

David was aged nearly five and spent $9\frac{3}{4}$ hours at the minder's. He arrived at 8 a.m. He hadn't seen the minder's son, aged 5, for three weeks over the holidays and they were both very excited, talking to each other. At 8.30 the other minded child arrived, and at 8.45 they all left the house to take the minder's son to school. The minder and the two minded children went on to the playgroup where they all spent the morning, the minder being a helper. They got back at 12.15 and the two children played in the dining room while the minder got a snack lunch ready. They helped her clear it away. Then they all listened to *The Archers* and all watched *Watch with Mother* ('It's our special routine'). From 2 to 2.30 she read to them; then the other minded child was collected. The minder and David went out for a walk with the dog – 'We talked to each other' – and collected the minder's son from school. They all had a biscuit and a drink together, and the two boys played in the sitting room while the minder got the dinner ready in the kitchen. At 4 they watched television for forty minutes. Then they all picked up the toys together. The minder's husband came home at 5 and they all chatted together. At 5.30 David's mother arrived and chatted to the minder for a quarter of an hour before they left.

These minders who played actively with the children did not seem to differ from other minders in the domestic pressures on them: their families were just as large, they as often had under-fives of their own, and they were just as likely to have more than one minded child to look after. Nor, interestingly, were they more likely than other minders to have had playgroup or other relevant training or experience or to express an interest in knowing about children's play. Nor was there any difference in the ages of the children they minded.

However the children did tend to have a shorter day with them. Two fifths spent less than six hours at the minders' compared with only one fifth of those whose minders did not play actively with them. (Even so, over half those who were played with had been there more than six hours.) In other words there were signs that the longer the child was at the minder's the *less* likely he was to be played with by the minder.

It is difficult from these varied accounts to make a succinct summary of 'a child's day at the minder's'. In general, however, they did not conform to the picture of confined inactivity portrayed by some other investigators. Far from being kept in one room and meeting no-one, three quarters of the children had been taken out at least once on the previous day, and in the last week a third had been taken to a park or playground at least three times. A quarter had been to a playgroup yesterday, and two fifths had been to visit or been visited by the minder's relatives and friends who often had young children too. In the London study less than half the children had been out on the previous day: indeed it is hard to imagine how some of the London minders *could* have gone out towing four, five, six or more small children.

While it is not easy to find comparable studies of children with their mothers, it seems likely that the child's activities at the minder's do not differ markedly from most children at home with their mothers. One study of London families with preschool children found that a sizeable hunk of 'yesterday', probably about half the waking day, was spent in play, 90 per cent of which was 'general' unspecified play, while 10 per cent was 'specific play' which included looking at books, listening to stories and music, and watching television, as well as conversation and physical contact. Much shorter periods of time were spent on shopping (including walks) and visiting (including playgroups). Only about 15 per cent of waking time was spent in 'concentrated interaction' (defined as 'being absorbed in what they were doing together to the exclusion of other activities') between mother and child (Lawson & Ingleby, 1974).

Outings and visits, while they may provide variety and excitement for the child, do not necessarily do so, and may equally be tiring and frustrating. About half the children's outings 'yesterday' in our study were routine trips to schools and so on, and some children seemed to be spending inordinate amounts of time in the wake of the minder's own complicated journeyings between shops, launderettes, nurseries and schools – to the extent that the children had little time left for play of any kind. Similarly, entertaining, or visiting relatives and friends commonly took the form of adults' chats over cups of coffee while the children played, often in a separate room or the garden. These visits some-times seemed to fill up what little spare time the minder might have had from her domestic chores for doing things with the children.

We would single out here a small group of eight children (12 per cent) who seemed to have regular and very affection-ate relationships with the minder's parents or parents-in-law. These relatives treated the children rather as grandchildren, and the children would call them 'gran' or 'grampy'. This affectionate relationship was even more noticeable with the minders' husbands whom we consider next.

Minders' husbands

The minder's husband, as we saw in Chapter 5, played a not insignificant role in the minding scene. Nearly all the chil-dren saw him from time to time, and over half saw him on most days they went to the minder. These encounters were often a good deal more than passing glimpses. Most of the husbands were said to play with the children (one fifth had actually done so yesterday), and nearly a third took them on outings. Some also did standby minding if their wives were ill or wanted to go out.

Sometimes things went a good deal further than this. A third of the husbands were reported as having a great affection for the minded children and spending a considerable amount of time with them. This was, not surprisingly, related to the amount of time the child spent there, since the paths of child and minder's husband would be unlikely to cross except very early in the morning or late in the afternoon unless the husband worked shifts. Nearly half of the children minded full-time had close and extensive relationships with their minders' husbands, compared with only 13 per cent of the part-timers. We give an example, picked at random from the group with especially good relationships, as an illustration:

> Susan was an only child, aged nearly five, who had been going to the same minder since she was a baby. She was a very lively and sociable little girl who was minded full-time and had become virtually one of the family, often staying the night several times a week because she liked being with the minder's three sons, one of whom was the same age. The minder's husband was described as loving Susan, and he saw a great deal of her – for an hour every morning, most lunch times and often in the evening too. He played with her in the same way as his own children, piggy-backs and general frolicking. On the previous day she had spent a quarter of an hour romping with him on the bed before breakfast (she arrived each morning at 7 a.m.), and he had joined all the children for a picnic lunch in the park and had played games with them. He had spent more time with her in the garden in the evening.

We wondered whether children without fathers might be more likely to have such a relationship, and we found this was indeed so. Out of the ten children with no father, six, or 60 per cent, had a very good relationship of this kind, compared with only 25 per cent of those with a father. This was not because the children of single mothers were more often minded full-time, since the same proportion – half – of those with and without fathers were full-timers. However, the higher likelihood of children without fathers having a special relationship with the minder's husband only held for the children minded full-time. The numbers are very small, but *all* the five full-time, fatherless children had, compared with only 10 (37 per cent) of the 27 part-time children with fathers.

Here then is a kind of 'bonus' for some full-time minded children, and especially for one of the more vulnerable groups of children.

The picture of life at the minder's emerging so far would seem to be rather better than has previously been found in inner city areas. Most minded children in Oxfordshire are cared for in pleasant surroundings, with freedom to play in most of the house and garden, and are also taken out. Most have reasonably good toys to play with, by and large as good as those provided by their own parents. Most also have the chance to play with other young children, and to meet older children and adults; indeed, most of the three- and four-year-olds go some mornings to a playgroup. And yet there are not too *many* under-fives at each minder's. Almost half the children are only being minded part-time, which many people would regard as preferable from the child's point of view. On the other hand some of the full-time children seem to have the advantage of particularly close relationships with the minder's husband, and this is especially so for those who do not have fathers of their own. Most of the children have not been farmed around from minder to minder, and a sizeable minority seem to be with minders who are unlikely to give up minding suddenly.

On the negative side there are signs that some children may be taken out too much, perhaps experiencing rather tiring, frustrating days with little time for play. There are also signs that most minders do not spend time doing or making specific things with the children, and there is also a tendency for children who are minded all day to be played with *less* than children who are only part-timers.

It is also important not to overlook the minority of children who are not in such favourable circumstances. Whatever measures we look at, somewhere between a fifth and a third of the children are faring less well, and there is a substantial minority for whom there is little cause for complacency. In particular there were about 16 children (24 per cent) who seemed to lose out on most counts. All of these children had restricted, cramped play areas or restrictions on messy play (and usually both), and had not been taken out much or at all in the last week; all but two had a very poor selection of toys, and twelve of them had only a small yard to play in or else no garden at all. Furthermore, 13 had neither played actively with the minder yesterday, nor had a close relationship with her husband, and eight had no other under-fives to play with. Eleven of these 16 children were minded full-time.

On the surface, then, with these important reservations, the picture of life at the minders' looks good for the children. In the next chapter we will turn to the question of whether they seem to be thriving in the midst of all this, and what sorts of relationships they have with their minders. Is all really as well as it seems?

8

The minded child: is he thriving?

At least as important as physical comfort, or toys to play with, is the quality of the relationship between each child and his minder. Warmth, affection, encouragement and understanding may mean more to a young child than whether he is taken out or has a garden to play in or is given lots of toys. In the case of minding this is particularly relevant, since minding is often said to offer the child more by way of close emotional bonds than do other forms of day care. In this chapter, therefore, we shall try to assess the quality of the relationship between minder and child. To do this we shall draw on what the minders said to us, but we shall also draw a great deal on what we ourselves saw – how the minder and the child behaved, and how they interacted with each other. As we go along we shall also compare the child's behaviour with his behaviour at home with his mother.

In one sense, of course, relationships cannot be measured; it is not possible to sum up such complex entities as human interactions and feelings. On the other hand there is little doubt that we all do make judgements about other people from what they say and how they behave, and there are ways of doing this reliably.

One way is to count the occurrence of certain 'events', which can be reasonably precisely defined and from which one can make inferences about underlying feelings and attitudes. We selected eight such measures, seven derived from the minder's (or mother's) behaviour towards the child or the things she said about him, and one from the child's behaviour towards her. These were: (1) praising the child at least twice; (2) caressing him at least once; (3) giving a detailed picture of his behaviour, character or development (at least three different statements); (4) giving a detailed account of his interests (at least three different ones or one persistent one); (5) expressing sympathetic awareness of his particular needs, feelings or problems (at least one remark); (6) having spent time actively involved with him yesterday; (7) not speaking slightingly about him (not more than one negative remark). We can also measure (8) the number of approaches initiated by the child towards his minder or mother, including any attempts to attract her attention. These are listed only briefly here as they have been described in detail in Chapter 2.

In addition to these measures, we also recorded systematically our overall subjective impressions of each child's behaviour during the interview, noting in particular what he was doing during the first twenty-minute observation period and for the rest of the time, and how much notice he took of the minder or of other children present. We also rated on a five-point scale the warmth shown by the minder or mother to the child; this was based both on what she said about him and on her behaviour towards him, including her tone of voice, facial expression and so on.

These, then, were the measures. We now turn to the results.

The minder's attitude to the child

We have grouped together in Table 8.1 the seven measures of the minder's behaviour and the warmth ratings. Three quarters of the minders praised the child, described his character in detail or did not speak slightingly of him, and two thirds described his interests in detail. Many were well above our minimum requirements for these measures: for example, nearly a quarter said five or more nice things about the child. Similarly, some of the descriptions of the child as a person were very rich and sometimes poignant. We selected four at random from the 11 fullest as illustrations:

He's very friendly; not aggressive – he hates being hit; doesn't play well; very intelligent; lovely little boy

	Minders* (N = 62)	Mothers† (N = 62)	London‡ minders (N = 39)
	Percentage Yes	Percentage Yes	Percentage Yes
Praises child's behaviour/manner at least twice	76	94	56§a
Caresses or kisses child at least once	47	82§b	49
Gives detailed picture of child's character etc.	76	82	69
Gives detailed account of child's interests	66	85§c	
Shows sympathetic awareness of child's needs or problems	36	26	
Was actively involved with child yesterday	52	68	64
Makes less than two hostile remarks about child	74	68	
Warmth rating (mean)	3·54	3·92¶	

* These figures exclude four minders where the child was not present.
† These figures exclude one mother whose child was not present.
‡ These figures are taken from Mayall and Petrie (1977).
§ Test of significance Chi Squared. a = P<·001; b = P <·01; c = P<·05.
¶ Test of significance t test. P <·05.

Table 8.1 *Percentage of minders and mothers scoring on measures of relationships with children*

but not quite right – he walks around sucking his thumb and doesn't like cuddles or kisses. He's a bit like a little adult.

She's a chatterbox: lively and bright and very loving – she likes an extra hug; demanding but quite adorable. I love her. She's a dear little soul. She eats very well and tells you she likes it.

She's very inward; she sulks; she doesn't adapt to other children – doesn't want to get to know them, not a friendly kid; not a happy child. Unsettled, just wants to follow me around. She's someone you don't want to get emotionally involved with; she needs too much security.

He's quiet. Intelligent but slow in actions. He enjoys playing with other children – gets quite excited [with them]. He's a gentle little boy and gets easily pushed around. Got a nervous disposition – if I tell him off he wets himself. He doesn't do naughty things, not like mine.

About half the minders caressed or kissed the child during our visit, and half reported having spent time actively involved with him yesterday. (This latter figure is higher than the 30 per cent quoted in the last chapter because here we include any unspecified reports of 'playing' or doing things together, however vague.)

Table 8.1 also shows how the mothers fared on the same measures, and this provides a useful yardstick for considering the minders. Significantly more of the mothers touched or kissed their children during their interviews (and the mothers' interviews were on average quite a bit shorter than the minders'), and significantly more of them gave a detailed account of the sorts of things their children were interested in. Also, taking each child's mother and minder, their mothers were rated as showing significantly more warmth to them than their minders. Even so, nearly half the minders showed as much (or as little) warmth to the child as the same child's own mother did.

On the other items the differences were not significant, although they generally favoured the mothers. Somewhat more minders than mothers (though a minority of both) expressed a sympathetic awareness of the children's needs, although this, too, was not a significant difference. These remarks, when they were made, tended to be concerned with children's difficulties, and it may be that minders were commenting from the outside on things the mothers took for granted, or which perhaps they did not recognize as problems.

The differences that were significant were probably only to be expected in the sense that it would have been very much more surprising if the mothers had caressed their children *less* often or shown *less* warmth than the minders. Much more noteworthy is the fact that the minders were not appreciably less perceptive of, and did not show noticeably less esteem for, the children than the mothers, and that many minders *did* seem to be warmly involved and interested in them.

On the other hand much depends where one puts the emphasis. Quite large numbers of minders did *not* do these things: one quarter praised the child only once or not at all (eight children had nothing nice said about them); a quarter also said disparaging things about him, and five minders made seven or more such remarks; a quarter gave only meagre descriptions of the child, and a third did so of his interests. Moreover, half the minders did not touch the child affectionately, and half had not spent any time actively involved with him yesterday. Two thirds did not say anything which indicated sympathetic understanding of his needs or problems. Only four minders scored positively on *all* the seven measures, and seven minders scored only on two or even fewer.

The child's behaviour

Approaching minder and mother

All but seven of the 62 children we observed at the minders' approached their minder at least once during the twenty-minute observation period, and all but five of the 62 we saw at home approached their mothers. It will be remembered that an approach included not only going up to the adult but attracting her attention in other ways such as calling, crying and looking at her. However, the children made significantly more approaches to their mothers than their minders (see Table 8.2). On average they made 6·5 approaches to their mothers but only 4·4 to their minders. In the Thomas Coram study the London children made an average of 6·2 approaches to their mothers, so in this important respect we can say that the two sets of children are comparable. However, the London children made far fewer approaches to their minders – only 1·2 on average.

Approaches	Minded child to mother		Minded child to minder	
	Number	Percentage	Number	Percentage
None	5	8·5	7	11·9
1–5	26	44·1	33	55·9
6+	28	47·5	19	32·2
Total	59	100	59	100

Table 8.2 *Number of approaches towards mothers and minders in 20 minute observation period**†

* These figures exclude seven cases where the child was not seen with both minder and mother.
† Test of significance: Chi Squared. P <·01.

One of the pivotal findings in London was the authors' impression that the minders' own child made more approaches to her than the minded child did, although her own child's approaches were not actually counted. From this impression they inferred that minders were not generalizing their motherly skills to minded children. We did count the minders' own children's approaches, but our results were not the same. There were 26 minders whose own child under five was present, and these children did not make significantly more approaches to the minder (their mother) than the minded children did. Indeed they were very similar, an average of 3·0 for the minder's own child and 3·6 for the minded child, and it was not uncommon for the two children to be playing together during the observation period and to come to the minder as a pair.

The generally lower level of approaches when the minder's child was there suggested that the presence of *any* other child, whether the minder's own or another minded child, might affect the amount of interaction with the minder. It can be seen from Table 8.3 that this was so. It can also be seen that the significant difference in approaches to mother and minder disappears. In other words this difference can be explained by the fact that children are more likely to be with another child at the minder's.

	Child seen alone		Child seen with others	
Approaches	Mean	Number of children	Mean	Number of children
To mother	7·1	41	4·9	21*
To minder	5·4	28	3·3	34†

* Test of significance: t test. Not significant.
† Test of significance: t test. P <·05.

Table 8.3 *Mean numbers of approaches to mother and minder when child is alone/with other children. (These figures exclude seven cases where the child was not seen with both minder and mother)*

However the effect of another child's presence was not quite the same at the minder's and at home, as can also be seen from Table 8.3. While a child made fewer approaches in both situations if another child was there, the effect was greater at the minder's. One likely explanation for this is that the other children at home were usually his own brothers and sisters, and therefore in competition for their mother's attention. They also tended to be a little older, since many of the home interviews were held at week-ends when school-age children were at home, and we did include siblings up to the age of seven.

We also looked at a number of other possible influences on the frequency of a child's approaches. One of these was his acquaintance with the minder before he started going to her. There was no evidence that the 25 children who went to minders they knew already made more approaches (see Table 8.4). On the contrary, they made slightly fewer, although not significantly so.

Another possible influence was the length of time the child had been going to the minder. Some writers have suggested that children initially make many demands but that these subsequently subside. We did not find any clear evidence that this was so: the nine* children who had been with their

* Excluding one child who was not seen in both settings.

	Already knew minder (N = 25)		Did not know minder (N = 37)	
	Mean	Number	Mean	Number
On own at minder's	4·7	13	6·0	15*
With other children at minder's	2·4	12	3·4	22

* Test of significance: t test. Not significant.

Table 8.4 *Mean numbers of approaches by children on their own and with other children, whether they already knew the minder when they started or whether they did not*

minders under a month made an average of 4·6 approaches (and 5·8 to their mothers) compared with 4·5 (and 7·0) for those who had been going for three months or longer. However, there was an indication, albeit from very small numbers, that in the second month the number of approaches did drop: the five children who were in their second month there made only 2·4 approaches on average to minders – but their approaches to their mothers were also reduced, to 2·0. While we cannot deduce much from such small numbers, it may be that this second month is a difficult one for the young child who is coming to terms with being away from home. It certainly seems likely, from what we know of the effects of separation, that there will be some process of change and adaptation. For example, Schaffer (1977) mentions three phases commonly found in children experiencing total or prolonged separation such as being admitted to hospital or taken into care: distress, despair during which he becomes quiet and apathetic, and finally detachment.

We also related the number of approaches to the age of the child, the number of hours he spent at the minder's, and to whether there were other adults present, but we found no significant connections.

Children making no approaches to the minder

We looked in greater detail at the 19 children who took virtually no notice of the minder at all (that is, those who never approached her or did so only once) and they emerged as rather different from the other children in important ways.

In the first place the effect of being with another child did not hold for these children, since nine of the 19 were on their own and ten were with another child. Secondly, those who were with other children very rarely played with them, and were significantly less likely to do so than the children who approached their minders more often. (See Table 8.5).

| | Number of approaches | | | |
| | 0 or 1 | | 2 or more | |
	Number	Percentage	Number	Percentage
Plays with other child at least once	3	30	19	73
Does not play with other child at all	7	70	7	27

Table 8.5 *Numbers of children making less than two approaches to their minders, whether they played with other children present during the observation period, or whether they did not* *†

* These figures exclude children on their own at the minder's.
† Test of significance: Chi Squared with Yates correction. P <·05.

It looks, then, as though these children who did not approach their minders may have been having difficulties generally in making relationships with others. As we shall see later, there is reason to think this may have been so, since many of them had rather poor relationships with parents too. However, this possible difficulty was not reflected in any characteristic pattern of approaches to their *mothers*. Most were somewhere around average, but four made only one approach, or more, to their mothers, while four made exceptionally many, including the most demanding child we saw who approached her mother 39 times in the twenty-minute observation period.

How involved is the child in things and people around him?

The child's spontaneous approaches to his minder or mother are only one very specific aspect of his behaviour. We were also interested in other aspects: for example, what he chose to do, whether he played with toys or with other children,

| | At minder's | | At home | |
	Number	Percentage	Number	Percentage
Dominant activity				
Doing little/nothing	7	12	2	3
Interacting with adult	11	19	29	50
Interacting with peers	10	17	3	5
Playing with toys	21	36	9	16
Physically active	5	9	11	19
Other	4	7	4	7
	58	100	58	100
Mobility				
Physically constrained (pram etc.)	2	3	2	3
Physically free but child stays put	21	36	10	17
Free and moving	14	26	16	28
Free and moving out of room too	21	36	30	52
	58	100	58	100
Significant proportion on minder's or mother's knee	11	19	24	41

Table 8.6 *The child's behaviour at the minder's and at home during the observation period**

* These figures exclude eight children where complete information in both situations was not available.

whether he moved about and left the room, or whether he stayed in one place and did nothing very much. Some of this behaviour we rated at the end of the observation period, and our results are shown in Table 8.6.

Looking at the child's dominant activity, we can see that the patterns were rather different at the minder's and at home. At the minder's he was most likely to play with toys, and to a lesser extent with other children, and was four times as likely to be rated as 'doing little or nothing' (12 per cent of those we observed compared with 3 per cent at home). At home he was more likely to be interacting with an adult (nearly always his mother) or, quite frequently, to be rushing around being physically active. This latter was even more obvious in the rating of mobility. Four fifths were on the move at home, and over half left the room, while at the minder's over a third stayed sitting where they were. Twice as many children spent some considerable time sitting on their mothers' knees as on their minders' knees.

These ratings suggest that the children were being more physically active, more socially involved, and were spending less time sitting around doing nothing at home than at the minder's. They do not, however, give a very rich account, and they leave out all sorts of relevant information, for example, about non-verbal behaviour or about the child's subjective experiences which give meaning to his behaviour. For example, does he derive equal pleasure from his minder's and his mother's knee? Does his absorbed play with toys indicate interest in the activity, or avoidance of something else? Does drowsiness imply tiredness, or escape?

Since we could not ask the children about their feelings, we had to try to infer feelings and meanings from what we saw, and to do this we used the detailed description of behaviour recorded systematically by the interviewer at the end of the interview. On the basis of these we divided the children into groups according to whether the picture was predominantly one of activity and involvement or passivity and detachment, both at home and at the minder's. We ended up with three groups:

The 'lively' group

We chose this name as best encapsulating the active, sociable and lively behaviour of the children in this group *both at home and at the minder's*. Seventeen children (29 per cent of the 58 children seen awake both at home and at the minder's) fitted this pattern, and we give some examples quoted from the interviewer's notes.

At minder's	*At home*
A happy, self-confident child mostly playing pretend games with the minder's child. Played well together	An attractive little girl, very friendly and independent. Mostly playing in the garden with friends, but ran in for a cuddle now and then
A tubby little girl who seemed cheerful and lively. Spent most of interview playing with minder's son – they chatted endlessly to each other	Seemed a well-adjusted, open, intelligent, busy little girl – made a lot of demands of her mother
A very jolly, cuddly baby, on floor most of time, physically very active, approaching minder, smiling and gurgling	A lively, alert and demanding baby; spent most of observation on mother's knee
Seemed a very happy, self-confident child and spent most of her time playing rather tomboyishly with minder's sons. Physically very active. All in garden and ran over to minder every now and again to talk to her	Played with toys quite busily but stayed close to her mother at first. Chatted away to her mother. Approached her mother a lot, and they cuddled. Later a friend came round and they rushed upstairs to play – coming down at intervals to mother
Totally busy and absorbed in playing with toys and other children . . . terribly busy and active the whole time, running about; made lots of approaches to minder	A delightful child, very active; climbing on and off father's lap; not a lot of toys but played with them and with brother busily; seemed happy and bright
Got on fantastically well with minder's child, who was older (hardly seen two kids playing so well); they played around the minder with toys and talking to her	A delightful, lively active toddler (16 months), very cuddly and affectionate and quite demanding. Mainly interacting with mother and playing with toys

Hard to believe she was only two; very advanced and speaking very fluently and clearly, and playing very constructively . . . a charming extrovert child, mostly playing with toys and interacting with minder

Very active – lots of approaches to mother, and cuddles; mainly interacting with other children and physically active rather than playing with toys

The 'quiet' group

In this group the children were characteristically rather detached and inactive. They did nothing very much, or were occupied in repetitive, solitary play, *both at home and at the minder's*. There were fifteen children (26 per cent) in this group. Examples are:

At minder's

A thin, pale child with a nervous tic of the head and very indistinct speech. Took no notice of the minder and did not approach her at all. Spent the time doing nothing very much, but did play with a visiting child some of the time

At home

Rather a sad little boy. Spent most of the interview on his mother's knee and not interested or involved in anything; hardly spoke

Sitting on floor arranging cars in obsessionally straight lines . . . spent almost whole interview doing this, took no notice of me or the minder, said nothing throughout except once to repeat a long word he liked the sound of, and made no approaches to the minder except once to get trouser button done up

Very absorbed in play most of the time – hardly approached his mother at all – his play was very concentrated . . . seemed sure of himself and self-contained

She was very quiet and rather subdued. Sat next to minder drawing, but no contact between them at all. Made no demands except to ask for milk. Quite independent – went off on own too

She seemed tired and listless. Spent the interview lying on the floor with a cushion or on her mother's or father's lap. Did not play with toys

A very solemn, quiet four year old – tried to play with the other children from time to time but not very successfully. Mainly doing little or nothing, not involved; did not make demands on minder

A quiet little boy, not playing with anything, but he came to his mother several times and sat on her lap for a bit. His older siblings were much more noisy and demanding

A quiet child playing very intently with his cars; hardly said anything to the minder, and no physical contact at all. He got on with playing without reference to her in any way

He played rather aimlessly with conkers. Played silently. Only approached his mother once, and seemed to ignore her. Did not speak at all during interview

A very, very quiet little girl but seemed happy and at home at minder's. Did little or nothing but virtually no toys to play with. She had brought a crayon from home but had no paper

Rather a moany, demanding child – spent most of observation period on mother's knee whining. Did not play with toys – but did not have many toys anyway

She did not open her mouth while I was there and seemed totally uninterested in me or minder. Doing puzzles repeatedly, very complicated ones and seemed advanced for her age. Her mother was expected, and every time a car drove past she looked up expectantly, but when her mother did arrive she showed no interest. Just didn't seem to respond to anything

She was an attractive child – very aimless at first; mainly doing little or nothing and not involved. Did not make demands on her mother nor approach her. Played with some toys a bit later and watched television

The mixed group

In this group the children were, as the name implies, a mixture of the other two, 'lively' in one situation and 'quiet' in the other. This was always in the direction of being *lively at home* and *quiet at the minder's*, never the other way round. This was the largest group, with 26 children (45 per cent). Examples were:

At minder's

Little boy aged 19 months – tended to ignore the minder – had very few toys and spent the interview not doing much on the floor – later went in garden and stayed there on his own, digging

At home

A lovely little boy . . . physically active and busy playing with birthday cards; constantly going to his mother and bringing her things

Seemed rather bored – she stayed sitting on couch doing little or nothing. She later went in the garden on her own

Seemed absolutely happy – far noisier and more relaxed than at minder's. Spent time playing with toys and moving round her mother – in and out of room but always back to mum

A pleasant child, but lethargic and inactive and hardly spoke. Mainly not doing much, very quiet and watching the minder. Later became sleepy and sat on her lap

Totally different at home – playing very busily all the time whereas at the minder's he'd just sat on her lap and hardly spoke. He was chatty, laughing and very bright – very busy with toys: a screwdriver and wires and some Lego. Seemed very advanced. Approached his mother quite often

She spent some of the time sitting on the minder's knee, but when put down she sat limply on the sofa sucking her thumb and looking dreadfully miserable – doing little or nothing most of time

A bright, energetic, rather cheeky girl – in and out of garden and going to her mother. Not playing with toys much, but physically active

A timid, quiet, nervous little boy, a very nervous way of talking and puts his hand in front of his mouth as if afraid people wouldn't listen. Very little confidence

He was lively, noisy, boisterous, showing off, tearing around and full of energy. [The interviewer described him as totally different.] Very responsive to his father, and talkative

A sad little boy, aged two years, nine months; spent the time sitting on the floor, mostly alone, while the other three children played with each other. Doing little or nothing most of the time, but also played with toys. Took little notice of minder and did not approach her

An attractive child: quite clingy to his mother at first and stayed on her lap or near her, but got more relaxed and later got more toys and made more noise. Constantly approaching his mother, showing her things, talking to her and so on

She was totally aimless – she did nothing all the time I was there; she looked terribly bored (aged four and a half). Seems very backward – speech is unclear and she's babyish. Dirty house, and child not allowed to use garden

A fine, bright little girl, very chatty, plump and bouncy. She was on the go all through, on and off sofa, in and out of room, bringing books, having cuddles with her mother

Overall, then, of the 58 children observed in both situations, 41 (71 per cent) were felt to be quiet at the minder's compared with only 15 (26 per cent) at home. This difference is highly significant. We can also put it the other way round: 74 per cent were lively at home, but only 29 per cent were lively at the minder's.

There are difficulties in interpreting these sorts of data that we should point out. First, we do not know how reliable our method of grouping children is. Secondly, our groups incorporate several different dimensions of behaviour, such as physical activity, sociability, play and talking, which may have both different origins and different consequences for the child. For example, our Quiet group included some children who were socially isolated but others who seemed to be less detached; it also included children who were involved in play, albeit often of a repetitive and obsessional kind, and others who were passive and did nothing at all.

There was some suggestion that the children in the Quiet and Mixed groups, although they were *all* quiet at the minder's, differed as groups along these lines, with the Quiet group being more often socially detached or playing concentratedly, and the Mixed group less cut off from the minder but more aimless and passive. About a third of the Mixed group were rated as predominantly interacting with the minder, but when we looked in detail at these nine children we found them to be rather sad, apathetic children who spent most of the interview just sitting not doing very much, often staying near the minder, even sitting on her knee, but in a distant way – not looking at her, not cuddling with her, not speaking, often with their backs to her, and not showing any pleasure in this closeness. So they were less detached than many of the Quiet group, none of whom were rated as predominantly interacting with the minder, but their contact was quite different from that of the children rated as mainly interacting with their *mothers* (many of them the same children) who were coming for cuddles, showing things, making requests, talking, and so on. In the Quiet group half were rated as mainly playing with toys, compared with a fifth of the Mixed group, and a third as playing in the concentrated, repetitive way we have described, compared with only two children in the Mixed group.

Our definition of 'Lively' also suffers from this problem. In particular it probably encompasses not only the relaxed and confident children but also those who were very anxious and insecure and who needed to go to their mothers for frequent reassurance. There were five children, for example, who approached their mothers very frequently during the twenty-minute observation period: two made 14 approaches, one 16, one 17 and one 39. One of these was in the Lively group and the rest in the Mixed group.

Another problem, which concerns not just the impressionistic data but all our observations of the child's behaviour, is its representativeness. Perhaps the child was having an off day, or was quieter than usual because the interview disrupted his normal activities – although there is no reason to think either would be more true at the minder's than at home. However, if it were so we would expect considerable discrepancies between our observations and the minders' descriptions of what the children were usually like. We had descriptions, usually very good ones, from their answers to the question 'What sort of child is he: how would you describe him to a stranger?'. We therefore looked at these in greater detail.

Mostly their descriptions were appreciative of the child or relatively neutral, but a minority, about 14 per cent, were rather critical and disparaging. Large numbers of minders used words which indicated quietness, detachment and passivity: these words included the following: quiet, placid, contented, easy-going, solemn, dreamy, adaptable, easy to please, passive, shy, reserved, no trouble, not naughty, moody, sulky, not friendly, inward, withdrawn. We did not include 'good' on its own, as it seemed too ambiguous. We give some random examples of descriptions we included as indicating 'quiet' children, and some we excluded as not being clear enough:

INCLUDED:

'*Very adaptable, very good;* tense over him holding his breath; very good – so good he only cries when tired; he's a dear; I'm very fond of him.'

'She's *good*; a nice *quiet* little girl; she does *sulk*; ever so *good*.'

'*Very placid*; very sweet and appealing; very lovable and *easy going*; beginning to be insecure; I get worried she's getting too *passive*; often wonder how happy she is.'

'He will *adapt to anything* really; *never any problem; placid;* always tired.'

'She's *pretty placid*; not a bad child to look after.'

'*Placid*, I would say.'

'He's a *good* little boy, *no trouble*; a bit *sulky* but I've *never had any trouble* – especially for a boy he's *no trouble*. I prefer girls.'

EXCLUDED:

'Very affectionate; good; you know, at times looks on us as parents.'

'A lovable little thing; he'll go to anybody; he's good tempered.'

'Very lively, not shy, into everything – I have to watch her all the time; pretty good child, very intelligent; gets over-excited; fussy with food; lovely manners.'

We can see from the top line of Table 8.9 the relationship between our groups and the minders' descriptions. Over four fifths of the Quiet group, three quarters of the Mixed group and less than a third of the Lively group were described by minders as 'quiet' or some similar word. This does strongly suggest that the quiet behaviour we saw in many minded children was not unusual, nor a result of our presence.

We should point out here that these two measures were not independent in the sense that our overall impressions of the child's behaviour could have been influenced by the minder's description of him. Only completely separate interviews and observations done at different times by different people could have ruled out this possibility. However, the ratings made at the end of the twenty-minute observation period *were* independent, since they were done well before the point the minder was questioned about the child, and we have already seen that our ratings and written descriptions were similar. So we do not think this sort of bias was very important in this case.

To some extent our three groups overlapped our previous measure of the number of spontaneous approaches the child made. As would be expected from our definitions, the children in the Lively group made more approaches to the minder than those in the other two groups, whether on their own or with another child, and only one did not approach his minder at all. However differences between the Quiet and Mixed groups were not significant, and two fifths in each group made only one approach, or none.

Faced with these large numbers of quiet children, with the fact that we know many of them are not quiet at home, and with the further fact that their quietness seems to be a constant feature of their behaviour at the minder's and not something peculiar to our interviews, what can we conclude? A number of questions come to mind. Is there something about these children or their homes which makes them like this? Or is there rather something different about the minders and the care they give these children? Or should we look for an explanation not in the children or the minders but in the structure of minding itself?

Are the quiet children different?

Amongst all the information we had on the background of the children we did not find very much that was related to quietness. We give a few of the more interesting figures in Table 8.7, where it can be seen that neither the length of time the child had been going, nor the number of hours he spent there, were associated with it; nor whether he had previously been looked after by someone else, nor whether his mother and the minder were friends before he started. However there were three variables that did distinguish the children: the child's age, the age at which he had started at the minder's, and whether he had home difficulties. We will consider each of these in turn.

	Quiet group (N = 15) percentage	Mixed group (N = 26) percentage	Lively group (N = 17) percentage
Age three or four years	80	43	24*a
Length of time at minder's less than one year	53	62	54*b
Hours per week at minder's less than 30	47	57	58*b
Age child started at minder's less than 30 months	53	38	12*a
Minder previously known to mother	40	42	35*b
Child had had previous caretaker	47	42	29*b
Child had home difficulties	60	62	29*c

* Test of significance: Chi Squared with Yates correction where necessary. a = P < ·001; b = Not significant; c = Quiet and Mixed groups combined, P < ·05.

Table 8.7 *Proportions of children in Quiet, Mixed and Lively groups, by the child's age and by various aspects of the minding arrangement*

Age and the quiet child

The quiet children were significantly older than the lively ones. Four fifths of the Quiet group were three or four years old, twice as many as of the Mixed group, but nearly four times as many as the Lively group. This was not because the quiet children had been going to the minder's for longer, but because they had started going when they were older. Over half were at least two and a half when they started (and more than a third well over four) compared with only 12 per cent of the Lively group. Nor is this, in its turn, due to their having been previously looked after by another minder or by someone else, since they were not significantly more likely to have had a previous caretaker.

We are left, then, with something of a puzzle. Why should the quiet children be older, and also have been older when they started? And why should this effect be even greater for the Quiet group than the Mixed group? One possible explanation is a developmental one: that liveliness diminishes with age. However, this does seem most implausible, and as far as we know there are no studies that support it. Another possibility might be that our expectations were different for the older children, but this is also unlikely since over half the three- and four-year-olds *were* observed as lively, either just at home or in both situations. A third possibility is that there is something about starting when a little older that makes it more difficult for the child to adjust to being away from home; however, it is usually said that separation effects are worse for younger children between about seven months and two and a half years.

We might also look for an explanation in the child's experiences at home. The older child, simply by having been around longer, may have experienced more – and more long-lasting – difficulties at home than younger children. There is also the possibility that minders find it more difficult to get on with the older starters, since they have not the same obvious need of physical attention as babies or toddlers.

Home difficulties and the detached child

What, then, about the child's home life? We asked systematically about a number of difficulties, such as divorce and separation, the children's ill health, and problems in relationships between parents and children. Other difficulties emerged unsystematically in the course of the interviews, including evidence of neglect or malnourishment (only counted if there was mention of a court case, or if an outside agency such as a doctor or social worker had been involved), mental illness in one or both parents (only counted if the parents themselves mentioned it), and marital difficulties

	Quiet group, (N = 15)		Mixed group (N = 26)		Lively group (N = 17)	
	Number	Percent-age	Number	Percent-age	Number	Percent-age
'Lone' parent	2	13	6	23	5	29
(Divorced/separated)	(2)		(5)		(3)	
(Unmarried)			(1)		(2)	
(Widowed)					(1)	
Child has poor relationship with parent	8	53	5	19	0	0
(with mother)	(6)		(2)		0	
(with father)	(2)		(3)			
'Neglect' of child	1	7	4	15	0	0
Mental illness in parent	1*	7	2†	8	0	0
Child's ill health	1	7	2	8	0	0
Other	1	7	2	8	0	0
Total number of families with at least one difficulty	9	60	16	62	5	29
Total number of families with two or more difficulties	4	27	7	27	0	0

* Both parents in this case.
† A further four probable cases are excluded.

Table 8.8 *Proportions of children in Quiet, Mixed and Lively groups with various kinds of home difficulties*

raised by parents. Table 8.8 shows their frequency in each of our three groups.

There are a number of very interesting points here, which concern not just differences between the quiet and lively children, but also differences within the Quiet group between the consistently Quiet and the Mixed groups. We will look at some of these in more detail.

Single parents

We included this as a category of difficulty because it now appears in official publications as a 'risk' factor, as, for example, in the DHSS study of local authority areas we quoted in Chapter 2. However, it is very clear from Table 8.8 that being the child of a single parent is not in itself associated with being quiet at the minder's. One has rather to look for differences between single parents, and we did find interesting ones. Seven of the eight single parents with children in the Quiet and Mixed groups were divorced or separated rather than unmarried, and in all but one case the home had broken up within the last year – usually under difficult or hostile circumstances. In at least two cases violence had been either used against the child or against his mother in front of him and in two cases it was the mother who had suddenly left home, abandoning the child to his father. In the Lively group, in contrast, there were only three divorces or separations, two of which had happened a long time ago when the child was very young. The third was a recent separation, and the mother had walked out, but there were special circumstances which may have helped: the father was rather unusual and was well able to 'mother' his two daughters; and the two girls were very close and went to the minder together. The other two single parents in the Lively group were a single mother who had always been on her own (so that her child had never known [or lost] his father) and a very recently widowed mother whose two young sons also went to the minder together.

Poor relationships with a parent

In a number of interviews it seemed to us that relationships between parents and children were not very satisfactory, and while this information was not always as detailed and reliable as we should have liked, we thought it was important to try to assess it. In evaluating these apparently poor relationships we used both what the mother said about how she or her husband got on with their child, and also for instance the number of disparaging remarks she made about him and what we observed about their behaviour together and her warmth towards him. We excluded a number who concerned us but without sufficient certainty. We give examples picked at random of the sorts of observations we included.

> 'We get on very well, but if I'm tired or miserable I do tend to reject him a bit – nothing terrible but he does annoy me. I don't have as much sympathy for him as I do for his [older] sister.' This mother did not make negative remarks about him, but she showed him very little warmth – rated only 1, the lowest point. There was also supporting evidence from the minder that the mother got on better with the older child and that she was rather neglectful of the younger one.

> Mother described father as 'not a loving sort of father – he works at week-ends – he's more interested in providing materially for her.' The child was aged three years, ten months.

> 'I get on better with him now than when he was tiny. I didn't like him much when he was tiny – found him too dependent.' In spite of this the child seemed rather detached from his mother and the interviewer described him as 'self-contained and old for his age' (which was four). He made only three approaches to her, and she said she felt a companion to him rather than a mother. The mother rated 3 on warmth.

> The father, in reply to how he got on with his child,

said 'He gets under me bloody feet.' And in answer to what sort of a child he was: 'A bloody nuisance.' This child, aged four years, nine months had a history of illness and may have been retarded. The interviewer wrote: 'It was clear the father couldn't stand him, and it was pathetic because the child wanted to please him so and kept going to him but he took no notice. He was very critical of him.'

'We get on pretty well really. [This child was aged two and a half.] She's strong-willed – never gone along with life. I'm not that patient. I give her attention but I don't make that into absorbed attention. Other people are so casual with their kids.' This mother said, of whether she enjoyed the child's bedtime: 'I don't go in for larking about – I'm terrified of breaking her routine. We were exhausted – never free of her.' As an advantage of working she said: 'That I can do things without being interrupted . . . and she [the child] can mix; she seemed so dependent.' This mother made nine negative remarks and was rated only 2 on warmth. The interviewer described her as '. . . a mum using a minder for relief from the child . . . who had obviously had great difficulty becoming a mother – motherhood was a real trauma.' There were hints that the child had been very difficult and aggressive.

'We have quite a good relationship now but it was very bad when he was a bit younger.' He was now aged two and a half, slept badly, and had tantrums. She had sought outside help from a social worker over this. Even so, she rated only 3 on warmth, and we included him because he seemed excessively demanding and anxious with her, making 39 approaches to her in the twenty-minute observation period.

'Yes, I like to see her gone; when she's grizzly I like to get her out of the way.' This was in answer to whether bedtime was enjoyable! The mother also said she didn't enjoy having her around, and at week-ends when she was not at work she put her to bed 'most of the day. I keep putting her back to bed – she'll have an hour or two in the morning if I'm lucky, then I put her back again once or twice during the day.' The mother made five negative remarks about her child, and was rated only 1 on warmth to her. The child was aged eleven months.

We can see from Table 8.8 that 13 children had rather poor relationships of this sort with a parent, or nearly a quarter of the sample. None of these children was in the Lively group. Within the other two groups they were significantly more likely to be in the Quiet than the Mixed group, not surprisingly, perhaps, when we remember that the Mixed group children were involved and lively at home, and that included being involved with their mothers. Even so five children in the Mixed group did have a poor relationship with a parent – but in three cases (compared with only two out of eight in the Quiet group) that turned out to be not with the mother but with the father.

We should also mention here that quite a few parents – six mothers and one 'single' father – in the Mixed group (though none were in the Quiet group) were noted by the interviewer to have particularly *good* relationships with their children. These included all five of the divorced or separated parents in this group.

Other difficulties

There was evidence that a small group of mothers were neglecting their children or abusing them. Three of these had become involved in legal action: none of the children in our sample had been taken into care, although one older sibling had been in the past. In a fourth case the family's general practitioner had been involved as the child was thought to be undernourished. The fifth case had not been substantiated in this way by an outside agency, but the minder described how the child had no clothes, was often brought half dressed, and she, the minder, had to buy clothes and food for him/herself. Although the numbers are very small, it looks as though these children were most likely to be in the Mixed group. Three of these five also had poor relationships with their mothers.

There were three families where we had good evidence of mental illness in the parents; in two of these the mother had left home, and in each case both parents had had a breakdown. The third case was a married mother. There were also four more families where mental illness was hinted at, all in the Mixed group.

Three of the children had had persistent illness involving hospital admission from time to time. One had asthma, one had severe eczema and was hyper-active, and the third was said to have some sort of arthritic disease. None of these other difficulties occurred in the Lively group; they were all found, albeit not in very large numbers, in the Mixed and Quiet groups.

It does look, then, as though the child's home life has something to do with how he thrives at the minder's. Three in five of the quiet children had at least one difficulty, twice as many as among the lively children. It is hard to avoid the conclusion that this is a causal connection, and that certain types of difficulty lead to certain combinations of behaviour at home and at the minder's. What sort of causal connection is less clear. For example, with the possible exception of children suffering from neglect, it is not at all clear that the mother's behaviour is the cause, since it is now widely accepted that mother–child relationships have as much to do with the child's behaviour towards the mother as the mother's towards the child. Nor is it clear why the child's behaviour at the minder's should be consistently quiet rather than, say, aggressive.

We should also remember that two fifths of the quiet children did *not* have any home difficulties, and that they comprised over half of those with no home difficulties, and over a quarter of the entire sample of children. Could there, then, be something about some of the minders and the way they treated the children that could explain the quiet behaviour?

Are the minders different?

The reader will recall that we asked each minder how long she had been minding, whether she had minded children before, whether she and the mother were friends, whether she had children of her own under five, whether she had relevant training or experience in child care, and so on. However, we could find no connection between their answers to any of these questions and the children's behaviour. Nor did amenities such as toys, gardens, outings,

	Quiet group (N = 15) Percentage	Mixed group (N = 26) Percentage	Lively group (N = 17) Percentage
Minder described child as 'quiet'	87	77	29*a
Minder touched child during interview at least once	13	50	65*a
Minder made two or more negative remarks about child	33	31	12*b
Minder made two or more positive remarks about child	60	81	82*b
Child has very good relationship with minder's family	0	12	29*c
Child seen with other children present	53	58	58*b

* Test of significance: Chi Squared with Yates correction where necessary. a = P <·001; b = Not significant; c = P <·01.

Table 8.9 *Proportions of children in Quiet, Mixed and Lively groups categorized according to how the minder described them or behaved towards them, and to whether they were seen with other children present*

playspace or playmates seem to have any crucial significance.

But when we turned to aspects of the *relationship* between minder and child we did find some important differences, as we can see in Tables 8.9 and 8.10. While the minders did not praise the quiet children less often than they did the other children, nor disparage them more, they were much less likely to touch them affectionately, they showed them less warmth, and also their relatives were less likely to have a good relationship with them.

These discrepancies were most marked for the Quiet group. Only two of the 15 children in this group had any affectionate physical contact with their minders, compared with half in the Mixed group and two thirds in the Lively group. The picture is similar for the warmth ratings, the children in the Quiet group having the least warm minders. We can also compare the minders' and mothers' warmth in Table 8.10. The mothers, too, showed less warmth to the quiet children, but they were not as cold as the minders were. Conversely, the minders showed just as much warmth to the Lively children as their own mothers did.

	Quiet group (N = 15)	Mixed group (N = 26)	Lively group (N = 17)
Mothers	3·5	4·1	4·1
Minders	2·9*a	3·5*a	4·1*b

* Test of significance: t test. a = P <·05; b = Not significant.

Table 8.10 *Mean warmth ratings for mothers and minders of children in Quiet, Mixed and Lively groups*

There are clearly problems of the chicken-and-egg variety in interpreting these findings. Do cold, unaffectionate minders produce quiet detached children? Or do quiet, detached and unresponsive children prevent minders expressing warmth and physical affection? It seems unlikely that either is wholly true. More probably, what we were rating was the interaction between minder and child. There were quite a number of the minders with quiet and detached children whom we felt to be pleasant, likeable, even warm women who were certainly capable of giving affection and often did so to their own children, but who nevertheless did not seem to manage it with the minded children in question. On the other hand, there were some – about a quarter in both the Quiet and Mixed groups, but also slightly under a fifth in the Lively group – who seemed generally to be cool and unemotional, or rather sad, apathetic women who did not like children much.

It seems probable, then, that the minders and children affected each other, so that the minders may have had difficulty showing, or perhaps even feeling, warmth and affection for children who, for their own private reasons, were detached and passive; each would decrease the emotional involvement of the other. Conversely an involved and responsive child would be rewarding to the minder, and their warm responses would be mutually reinforcing.

Did the child's behaviour worry the minder?

As a final indication of each child's behaviour we asked his minder about any problems she had had over his general behaviour and language in the last month over and above specific problems to do with eating, sleeping and toilet training. We found that, in spite of so many children being quiet, subdued and detached, the minders were not, by and large, worried about their behaviour nor about their language development. However 18 minders did mention problems, some of which sounded quite serious, and we therefore decided to assess more carefully how many children were disturbed or distressed or had language difficulties.

We included in our assessment only children for whom we had a reasonably specific and unambiguous description of behaviour. Under disturbance we counted reports of withdrawal, sitting without moving or speaking, tantrums, tics and, in one case, head-banging and rocking. Under distress we included almost constant crying, prolonged screaming when left, excessive clinging and a need for constant reassurance, or other signs of anxiety such as one child's continuously holding his coat. We give some examples, chosen at random, as illustrations:

> She used to be a bonny, bouncing baby but she's changed [since the recent loss of her father]. Now she's very solemn, moody and confused. She can't understand – she expects him to fetch her. She's now very anxious and worried, for instance if her mother doesn't look back when leaving or is late collecting.

> Very quiet and placid. At first she wouldn't talk for weeks and weeks – she just sat on the settee and didn't answer. A bit better now but her language is not good – difficult to understand.

> He needs an awful lot of reassurance; he's got it in his head his mother doesn't love him and I don't know what to say. He used to cry all day and still does some days. He has a stutter and a lisp.

> He's very withdrawn – you'll take that back to the office and say it's because he's being minded but it's not. He worries about his father hurting his mother or his baby sister – I don't know what to say to him. Also he rocks and head-bangs but not so much here now. He needs a lot of reassurance – to be told I love him. He's fiercely independent and tries not to show his feelings – it's terrible to see in a child that age.

On these criteria 13 children (20 per cent) were disturbed or distressed. They were equally likely to be quiet or lively children but with rather different problems in each group. The four in the Quiet group were all withdrawn children, and the four in the Lively group were all anxious but not withdrawn.

In estimating language backwardness we only included reports supported by both minder and mother, or problems which had come to the attention of social workers, teachers or other outsiders. On this basis we reckoned that eight children (12 per cent) definitely had language problems (and six of these also had behavioural difficulties).

Thus nearly a quarter of the children were reportedly showing disturbed or distressed behaviour, or language retardation, or both. There is little doubt in our minds that many of these children were very unhappy. Further, we have reason to think that the true prevalence of such problems may well be higher. Our observations would suggest that there were more children who were sad, passive, and withdrawn than were mentioned by the minders, and we excluded from the language estimate seven children (11 per cent) whose language was described as poor but about whom we felt the evidence was not sufficiently clear.

We cannot be sure that these estimates are reliable, since we do not know how good minders were at recognizing problems, and we did not use tests of proven reliability to assess the frequency and severity of the behaviour problems described. We do know, though, that the minders more often mentioned worries over children's behaviour and language than the mothers did; if we had used just the mothers' reports only four of the 15 children would have been identified as facing problems. This may have been because the children were behaving differently at home.

There was some evidence that mothers explained away signs of disturbance as normal development, as the following comments reveal:

> I'm not happy about her temper tantrums but they all go through it.

> She's getting very cheeky but everyone says it's just a phase.

> . . . about not sharing toys, but other mothers find the same thing.

A few mothers reported worries over children not mentioned by the minders as problems, but we did not consider any of these to be very serious. Some concerned bad habits or language which the mothers felt the children had picked up at the minders' and which irritated them; others were rather unspecified reports of being 'cheeky', 'naughty', 'difficult at times', and so on.

Given the large number of children in our sample, we felt that the amount of difficult behaviour reported, especially reported by mothers, was suprisingly small. But this may have been due to the fact that we did not ask about particular behaviour problems. Two studies of three-year-olds in London, which used a check-list of specific problems, certainly found a much greater prevalence of difficulties reported by mothers (Richman, Stevenson and Graham, 1975. Coleman, Wolkind and Ashley, 1977). In the one area where we, too, asked mothers specific questions about bedtime problems, we did get more problems reported. Twenty-three per cent of our mothers reported problems over children resisting going to bed, being difficult to settle, or waking at night. This does suggest that we may have underestimated behaviour difficulties generally.

Were the disturbed or distressed children different?

In looking at these children in detail we need to distinguish between the six whose behaviour seemed to indicate anxiety and dependency from the seven who were predominantly withdrawn (three of whom were also somewhat anxious). The main differences between these groups is that the anxious ones had all started at the minder's within the last six months (mean length of stay 4·1 months, range 1–9 months), while the withdrawn ones had been going much longer (mean length 12·4 months, range 3–28 months).

This would strongly suggest that the anxious children were showing distress at the recent separation from their mothers. Whether the withdrawn ones had originally been anxious, but were now in a later stage of adaptation, is less clear. Generally, though, minders reported very few difficulties when children started, as we saw in Chapter 4, and it seems unlikely that they would forget any *very* distressed behaviour in the early weeks.

We did not find other differences between the two types of problem children, but combined as one group they did differ from the other children in several ways. They were more likely to have home difficulties: all the children with language problems and 10 of the 13 with behaviour problems came from families with home difficulties, although no particular type of difficulty predominated. They were also more likely to have been older when they started going to their present minders: nearly two thirds had been virtually three years old, or more, when they started, compared with less than a third of the children without behaviour problems. This difference was statistically significant. Six out of the eight disturbed older starters had previously been looked after by someone else, two by relatives, two by minders and two in nurseries. This may suggest that the more difficult children get moved about more. Boys were also reported as having behaviour problems rather oftener than girls (32 per cent of the boys' behaviour worried the minders, but only 14 per cent of the girls'). There may be links here with other work showing that the effects of parental disturbance are worse for boys than girls (Rutter, 1971). It may also be that people's expectations are important, and minders may have found withdrawn and passive boys more difficult to accept than girls.

There does seem little doubt that the origins of the children's behaviour problems lie not in what happens at the minder's but in the home circumstances, as the minder we quoted above suggested (see page 193). However the children's difficulties are perhaps not helped, and possibly are even compounded, by minders who have little insight into the child's feelings: minders who see, for example, withdrawn behaviour as 'unfriendly' or 'sulky', or passive behaviour in a boy as 'sissy', or language problems as 'mumbling'; or who are themselves cold and indifferent to the children.

It is hard to quote exact figures, but we felt that perhaps six of the 15 children were with sympathetic, concerned and actively helping minders, while five were with minders who seemed aware of problems but were not doing anything particular to help. Four were with indifferent, cold, even somewhat hostile minders who seemed to show little understanding of the children and probably disliked them. We describe three of these below, and then three of the best ones:

Dean, aged two and a half, had a history of illness, and his speech was very backward. He had been with the same minder since he was a baby, and went to her 33 hours a week. His behaviour at the minder's was very quiet, withdrawn, aimless and unresponsive, but he was much more active at home and seemed to have a good relationship with his mother. The minder described him as 'not friendly, not for a long while . . . selfish but not through my fault, his older brother and sister were always made to defer . . . he's moody . . . a bit of a sissy.' She was quite a warm person but showed very little warmth to him. During the interview she made seven negative remarks about him and did not praise him at all. While she did not seem worried about his quiet behaviour, she was aware that his speech was not right and did try to get him talking.

Barry, aged nearly five, also had a history of childhood illness, and he had a nervous tic, very indistinct and backward speech, and tantrums. (The headmaster of the primary school had recommended speech therapy). He had been with the minder eleven months and went there 44 hours a week. He was described as pale, quiet and sad at the minder's and at home. He seemed to have quite a good, if subdued, relationship with his mother, but a very bad one with his father who was extremely critical and disparaging of him but whom Barry tried desperately to please. (The father was present for part of the interview.) The minder described

Barry as 'very difficult; very moody; he'll mumble; he likes playing on his own.' She was not a particularly warm person and showed little warmth to him. She made seven negative remarks about him and no positive ones, and she did not touch him. She was, however, aware that he was rather backward, and had tried unsuccessfully to discuss his speech with his mother.

Sandra, aged four and a half, came from a broken home. Her mother had walked out, and her father (himself rather depressed) looked after her and also her two older sisters. She went to the minder 35 hours a week, and had been going for ten months. She was left there on the first day never having met the minder before. For weeks and weeks she never spoke but just sat on the settee, and her language was very very indistinct. She had got a bit better recently but still usually replied 'I don't know,' to any question. The minder described her as 'very placid – not a bad child to look after – "Will you do this, Sandra?" – she'll do it.' The minder did not seem interested in her, nor indeed in children generally. She showed her no warmth at all and did not touch her; she neither praised her nor showed much hostility, apart from one hostile remark, and seemed indifferent. Yet Sandra was a Social Services priority child – they had found the minder and paid her. At some point they had also arranged speech therapy for her, and the minder was expected to take her to the clinic. She felt this was not fair on her own daughter so she refused. The Social Services Department made no alternative arrangements to get Sandra to the clinic, and they had not visited the minder in the last six months. The one redeeming feature in this drab picture was the relationship between Sandra and the minder's daughter who was the same age and who seemed to understand her speech. They played together, Sandra always following the daughter's lead.

In contrast, there were other minders who not only

showed considerable insight into the children's behaviour but who also managed to achieve quite good or even very good relationships with them; and there were a few whose commitment, thoughtfulness, and patience were remarkable. Again we give some examples, not randomly chosen but selected to illustrate these points.

Kevin, aged four, was the most disturbed child in our sample. He was minded part-time for 20 hours a week. When he first started at the minder's ten months ago he would rock and head-bang for long periods, and also smashed things and kicked. His home life was very disrupted, with a series of 'fathers' and a mother who had grown up in children's homes. His mother showed moments of great warmth and tenderness to him in the interview, but at other times was indifferent, even hostile, and he eventually went upstairs and had a head-banging session. At the minder's he was quiet and withdrawn, but also came to her and took her hand and talked to her. At first he just sat on the swing but she said she liked to let him do that for a bit when he arrived because he needed some peace and privacy. She was very concerned, warm and loving towards him, said a lot of nice things about him and did not make a single disparaging remark, and there seems little doubt that he liked being there and that she had helped him. 'He needs extra love afterwards – to be told I still love him even though I've told him off. He needs more reassurance than any I've had.' She described the pleasure of seeing him paint his first picture using bright colours instead of the black he usually chose. She felt he really needed to be in a nursery school where he could do more things and meet other children, but his mother did not want it.

Anne, aged nearly five, went full-time to the minder for 42 hours a week. She had been going there for six months but had not settled down. The minder described her as 'very inward; she sulks; doesn't adapt to other children, doesn't want to get to know them; not a friendly kid, not a happy child; unsettled; she just wants to follow me; she's someone you don't want to get emotionally involved with – she needs too much security.' She also said: 'She's not happy here – she just waits for her mother to come – she asks when she comes (in the morning) how many times the clock has to go round before Mummy comes.' Anne was so anxious that she did not even like to go out to the school to fetch the minder's child. The minder clearly found it an emotional strain looking after her, and had thought of giving up: 'I thought I'd stop having her because she's not happy, but then I thought her mother would only find someone else and that would be worse for Anne.' She had also gone to considerable lengths to think of ways to get through to Anne: 'I've been to their house for her to try to get to know me better but she's still very inward there and wouldn't talk to me – she talked to me through her mother.' At home Anne was much happier and more relaxed. She did not have a warm or close relationship with her mother who took the view that the child must learn to be independent of her, but her father showed her a lot of warmth. Her mother knew about Anne's behaviour at the minder's but did not see it as a problem; her main worry was that the minder might not want to go on having her.

Duncan was four and a half and lived with his father since his mother had left home. He went to the minder full-time (36 hours a week) and had been going for four months. At the minder's he was timid, nervous and lacking confidence, and sometimes he would cry all day. He had a stammer and would hold his hand over his mouth when talking. The minder described him as needing a great deal of reassurance because he thought his mother didn't love him. The minder was a very warm person who showed a great deal of warmth to Duncan and said a lot of nice things about him, and they had a good relationship. At home he was described as totally different: lively, noisy, boisterous, confident and full of energy, and he clearly adored his father; the interviewer noted that it was hard to believe it was the same child.

Are minders substitute mothers?

This chapter has been about the behaviour of minded children and their relationships with their minders. The first conclusion that we must draw is that these relationships are clearly not, for most children, close and satisfying ones. Three in five children seemed to be quiet and detached, or at least not very involved with their minders, and more than one in four were disturbed or distressed there or had impoverished speech.

Whatever the reasons for this, and we will consider some in a moment, we must seriously call in question one of the main advantages claimed for minding over other forms of day care, namely that it offers a child a rich, loving and satisfying emotional bond with one person, similar to the bond he has with his own mother, or even in some cases compensating him for the love he is failing to find at home. While, at its best, minding can offer this, and did to some of our children, it did not do so most of the time to most of them.

The explanation does not appear to be that minders are cold and unloving women, nor that they are indifferent to the children they mind. On the contrary, most of them seem to be warm, caring and kind people, certainly neither unloving nor unlovable; and most of them are appreciative of the minded children, and interested in them as people. Yet, despite being essentially well-disposed, they fail to get close to the children, and often do not give them much warmth or physical affection.

It seems probable that to some extent the children's detached and quiet behaviour stems from their home lives, since three in five of them were having difficulties there. When we look at the sorts of problems, and at what seems to 'buffer' some children from their effects, it is tempting to see them as fitting in with what others have found about the effects of separation. For example, Rutter has claimed that it is the discord within a marriage rather than the actual break-up of the home that is emotionally harmful to the child, and that the effects may be mitigated if the child manages to maintain a good relationship with one parent (Rutter, 1972). Another study showed that the adverse effects of separation through hospital admission are reduced if the child is admitted with a brother or sister (Heinicke and Westheimer, 1965). Other work has shown that repeated admission to hospital in early childhood is significantly associated with later disturbance, and also that children from disadvantaged homes show an increased vulnerability to stress (Douglas, 1975; Quinton and Rutter, 1976). Quinton and Rutter write: 'Both human and animal evidence shows that it is insecure and troubled individuals who are most likely to be damaged by stressful separation experiences.'

But it is less clear what is cause and what is effect in the home. For example, a mother may find it very difficult to get on with a child who has been difficult or fretful or a bad sleeper from infancy, or one who is persistently ill and whose relationship with her is disrupted by hospital admissions, or who is hyperactive. Such a child might even in his turn play his part in her depression and mental breakdown, even in her marital difficulties. Most of the circumstances we included as home difficulties, with the exception of neglect and cruelty, are open to causal interpretations in this direction as well as to the more usual explanation – that it is the parents' behaviour that affects the child.

If we seem to dwell on this point, we do so deliberately. Working mothers of young children already have to face considerable social disapproval, and it would be unfair both to them and to their children to add unnecessarily to this burden of guilt. It seems very likely that some children just are less attractive and rewarding to be with, and are more difficult to love, so that both mothers and minders find them more difficult to get on with. It is also likely that the mothers of such children may be more likely than other mothers to feel drawn to work outside the home.

The children who were detached and quiet at their minders' fell into two groups: those who were also like this at home, and those who were much more involved, active and lively at home. The former, about one in four of the children in the sample, differed from the rest in several other ways in addition to their quiet behaviour at home. In the first place they were older, and also older when they started going to the minder. Secondly the relationships with their minders seemed even less good than those of the other quiet children: their minders touched them even less often (indeed very rarely at all), and showed them even less warmth; and they were less likely to have close relationships with the minder's family. Thirdly, a number were more likely to be not so much inactive and passive as excessively absorbed in play to the exclusion of people. Finally their mothers, too, showed them less warmth than the mothers of the other quiet children, and more often had problems in getting on with them.

It seems difficult to avoid the conclusion that this group of children were, for whatever reason, having difficulties in forming loving relationships with others, and were in need of special help. We may draw two other conclusions about them. The first is that they would be unlikely to be any better off at home with their mothers since they did not seem to be markedly happier at home than at the minder's. Secondly, in view of their greater age (they were mostly three and four year olds), of their difficulty in relationships, and of their apparent interest in 'play' rather than 'people', minding would seem not to be the most sensible choice of care for them. It could be argued that they would be more likely to benefit from a more child-centred environment offering plenty of opportunity for stimulating play and a number of adults with whom they would not be expected to form very close emotional bonds.

Those children who were quiet both at home and at the minders' were a minority. The largest group of children, approaching half the sample, were also detached and quiet at the minders', but at home they seemed to behave in the involved, active and lively way one expects of young children (although a few seemed rather anxious and insecure judging from their very frequent approaches to their mothers). The majority of these children, too, had difficulties at home, but these more often involved the break-up of the marriage, with one parent leaving home (and thus leaving the child). On the whole the parents got on well with these children, and they showed them more warmth than the parents of the other quiet children; a number of single parents seem to have especially good relationships. The children's relationships with their minders, on the other hand, are not conspicuously successful. Their minders are a bit warmer and physically more affectionate to them, but still less so than the minders of children in the Lively group. The children played less with toys than those in the Quiet group, and many of them were rather passive – sitting around doing nothing very much, sometimes on the minders' knees.

It is difficult to know what conclusions to draw about this group of children. On the face of it, it would seem a solution for their mothers to stay at home with them, since the children seemed happier at home and got on quite well with their parents. However when one looks below the surface it is not at all evident that this would be best for mother or child. Many of these mothers were single and had either to work or to live on social security benefits – which brings its own problems. Many of them, too, were coping with a number of stressful life events, and recent work on the social origins of depression has shown that in such circumstances a job may be a crucial safety-valve, preventing depressive breakdown (Brown and Harris, 1978). Indeed, mental illness had already hit some parents in this group and was suspected in quite a few more. Furthermore, it is quite possible that the very good relationships we found between some mothers and children in this group were made possible just because the mothers did go out to work and got away from their children for a while.

There were also children, about a quarter of those in our sample, who seemed to be faring well, and were lively and involved both at home and at the minder's. Although one quarter is too few for complacency, it does at least show that some children can be minded without becoming detached or passive. On the whole they were younger than the other children, and, contrary to what one might expect (since separation is usually considered to be more harmful then) they were more likely to have started going to the minder when they were under two and a half. They had fewer home difficulties, and those they had seemed less disruptive and anxiety-provoking. They had good relationships with their parents, and seemed to feel secure enough at home to have the confidence to form warm relationships with others. They received a lot of warmth and physical affection from parents and minders, and the minders showed them as much warmth as their own mothers did. There were, however, exceptions: one or two minders in this group did not appear to be very warm, and one or two children did appear to be anxious and distressed at the minder's.

This brings us to the small, but not insignificant group of children, about one in four, who were disturbed or distressed at the minder's or had backward speech. They were found equally among our three groups, but those in the Lively group were all distressed, while those in the Quiet group were all withdrawn. They had started at the minder's at a greater age than other children, and tended more often to have been in some previous form of care. They were more often boys than girls. But what was most obviously different about them was that the anxious ones had all been going to the minder for less than six months, while the withdrawn ones had been going for about a year on average. This may indicate that early distress gives way, in time, to more subdued and resigned behaviour, and eventually in some children to disturbance and withdrawal. However, we are not sure that this is so.

We have so far avoided any discussion of whether the large numbers of quiet and detached children were unhappy, because we preferred to present a description of the behaviour we saw rather than an attempt to interpret it. In the case of the disturbed and distressed children we can reasonably say that they were unhappy: their behaviour spoke for them, and there was plenty of supporting evidence. However they accounted for only a fifth of the detached children, so what about the other four fifths? Can we assume that quietness, detachment and passivity are necessarily signs of unhappiness? Or that a child who is more quiet and detached away from his mother than with her is not happy?

We find ourselves here in something of a dilemma. These children were not showing the overt behaviour one might associate with unhappiness. They were not crying, screaming, whining, complaining, demanding, fighting, throwing tantrums or in any way fretting. Nor were they excessively or pathologically withdrawn. So we cannot say with absolute confidence that they were all unhappy. On the other hand they were certainly not behaving in the way one would expect happy, thriving children to behave, and we cannot, in all conscience, argue that there is no cause for concern. The danger signs are clear enough, and it would be doing minded children an ill service if we did not take them seriously.

Thus far we have suggested that the root of the minded child's detachment and quietness lies in the child and his home life and not in the minder and the care she gives the child. Given the problems we found, it is difficult to argue otherwise. However we should not forget that a minority of minders, perhaps a quarter, were felt to be cold, unresponsive people, sometimes rather sad and depressed or worn down by their own family problems. We should also remember that home difficulties do not account for all the detached children; quite a number had no home difficulties that we could discover, but were still detached or passive at the minder's.

There was also evidence that minders did not always recognize problems, or signs that the child was unhappy, and many of them failed to recognize detachment, passivity, apathy and even withdrawal for what they were. On the contrary they saw the children as very good, well-behaved and contented. It is possible that this lack of understanding on their part may have compounded the children's difficulties.

It is by no means certain, then, that the whole explanation lay at the children's doors, and one wonders whether there is not something about minding as such which encourages passivity in a child. In the next, and final chapter we shall look more closely at this, and we shall also consider minding in the context of alternative forms of care.

9
Conclusions

What have we learnt about minding as a way of caring for young children? Is there any evidence that will resolve the conflicting claims of its champions and its critics? Inevitably in such a small study we cannot find all the answers; indeed our results sometimes seem to raise more questions than they answer, and they certainly do not prove anybody right or wrong. There are no villains and no heroines, although there are some children who seem to be victims.

We have described a relatively prosperous, largely rural area where housing conditions are good in the main, and where there are no concentrations of the gross problems and deprivations that exist in some of Britain's large cities. Against this background we have talked about two groups of women who appear, on the surface, to complement each other: one group who want to go out to work and who need care for their children, and another who want to stay at home and would like to look after extra children along with their own.

The minders in general have good facilities for the children in the way of toys, playspace, other children to play with, and places to take them. Moreover they often like their minded children, take an interest in them and sometimes go to considerable lengths to help them. Often their husbands and other relatives take an interest in the children too. The children have not usually suffered repeated moves from one caretaker to another and their mothers seem satisfied with the care they are receiving. Many of the older children also go to playgroups.

All this sounds ideal, and one might expect the children to be happy and thriving. Yet we found only about one child in four whom we felt unequivocally was well-adjusted, active, socially outgoing, and boisterously playing in the way that young children should be. The great majority, some seven in ten, were noticeably quiet, detached and subdued at the minder's, and were not, we felt, thriving. Sometimes they seemed not to be thriving at home either, but more often they were lively and responsive at home and had a good relationship with their mothers, though their high spirits became muted at the minder's.

It is hard to know how unhappy all these quiet and detached children were. Quite a large proportion of them, two in five, did not approach their minders at all, and tended not to play with other children present, but they were not necessarily passive and apathetic, and some seemed totally absorbed in play – albeit of a rather repetitive and uncreative kind. Others appeared to be slightly less cut off from their minders, stayed near them, even sat on their knees, but in a passive and apathetic way with no sign of pleasure and enjoyment. Others seemed detached from their minders but did play with other children, although they usually took a passive, following role with the minders' own children. But even if we cannot say for certain that they were all unhappy, we can say that they were not conspicuously happy, and that their behaviour gives no grounds for satisfaction or complacency.

Cutting across these groups of lively and quiet children, we found another set of children, about one in four, who were quite clearly distressed or disturbed or had language problems, and there was little doubt that most of them were very unhappy.

Given the high concentration of home difficulties of one kind or another among the quiet and detached children, and also among the disturbed and distressed ones, we must conclude that a large part of the explanation for the children's behaviour is to be found in their homes, or at any rate outside the domain of their minders. Many of these children are experiencing considerable stress at home; some have been through difficult separations from one or both parents, whether through the break-up of the home or through their own ill-health and hospital admissions. They are likely to be highly anxious and vulnerable to further separation, even if this is temporary and they return home each day.

Yet are home difficulties the whole story? From our evidence we think not, although it is difficult to distinguish cause from effect. First there were quite a number of quiet children who did not apparently have home difficulties. Secondly about a quarter of the quiet children had minders who did not seem to enjoy minding and were cold and indifferent to them: it seems likely that children would not become attached to minders like this, although the explanation could be the other way round. Thirdly there were other minders who seemed to be warm and caring, and yet the children still did not seem to respond to them. We find this puzzling, because young children normally have little difficulty in becoming attached to any warm and loving adult, even if they do miss their mothers. It suggests that we may have got the wrong impression of the minder's usual warmth to the child. Finally there are features of life at the minder's, and features of the way minding is organized, that we believe are likely to increase anxiety and promote quietness, detachment or passivity. We will look at some of these in more detail.

The first is the abrupt way children are left with minders after very little preparation. Some children already know their minder (although this does not itself guarantee that they are used to being left with her), but the majority do not, and they may meet the minder only once or twice, briefly, before being left with her all day. Quite a number have never met her at all before they start. Sometimes the transfer is appallingly managed. We can recall the social services priority child whose mother had just walked out, and who was dumped by her father at the house of a minder she had never seen, where she sat for weeks mute and passive. Or the child who was picked up from her first day at nursery school by a minder who was a total stranger, and then taken to that minder's house. Since we came across only one or two children who had been gently eased into being left with a minder, we cannot show that it helped them to adjust, but it does seem likely that being unceremoniously dumped would make any child highly anxious. Some minders were critical of parents who did this, but they did not have any clear rules themselves for ensuring that it did not happen.

Not only do many children have very skimpy introductions to their minders and their houses, but when they are left on their first day their mothers rarely stay more than a few minutes with them, if at all. The majority of mothers and minders are agreed that it is much better for the mother to go straight off, and that her staying only prolongs the child's distress. One may wonder whether it is not rather the mother and minder who are spared an upsetting scene.

Behind their consensus on this is doubtless the fact that once his mother has gone the child stops crying. Yet it seems very unlikely that he stops feeling anxious just because his mother is out of sight. On the contrary it seems much more probable that his distress is not a generalized statement *about* his mother going, but a direct appeal *to* her not to go, so once she has gone there is no point in continuing to cry. We can also consider here the wider meaning to the child of what has happened. He protests; his mother walks out in the middle of his protests; he has failed to stop her. If this happens repeatedly he may come to feel that he has no control over his situation, that he is helpless to change it. Judging from findings on learned helplessness in recent years, it seems likely that he may become passive and resigned, even depressed. This sort of abrupt break may therefore contribute to the quiet child's behaviour at the minder's.

Minding is not the only form of day care where children experience this abrupt separation; some day nurseries and nursery schools also do not encourage mothers to stay. However there is evidence that this may be changing, and that some do now insist on a more gentle introduction, with mothers staying the first morning or so. And the playgroup movement is firmly committed to the principle that a mother should stay with her child until he is ready to separate from her without visible distress.

There may be other features of life at the minder's which have an effect. Having been abandoned by his mother in this unwanted situation, what does the minded child find? He may find it all totally strange and frightening and quite unlike his own home. Or he may find an ordinary house and garden much like his own, a supply of toys much like his own, and a sort of 'mum' organizing things much as his own mum does. On the face of it, it may look familiar, but is it? They are not *his* toys, *his* house, *his* mum. Even worse, there may well be another small child there whose home, toys and mum they are, who is territorially in charge, so to speak.

So there may well be important differences for the minded child. In the first place the power structure is different: he comes cap in hand, dispossessed. Everything belongs to someone else, often to another child whom he must appease. Secondly, the rules may well be different: he must learn anew what is permitted or forbidden, and these rules may not be consistent with those in his own home. Faced with these differences, the apparent similarity with home may actually be confusing rather than helpful, and increase his feelings of anxiety and inadequacy.

When all this comes on top of disrupted home circumstances which have already undermined his sense of security, or where he has already experienced failure in his relationships with his mother or father, the situation may be even more confusing and threatening. He may find himself in a predicament alarmingly similar to the home which is giving him so much anxiety, and he may well react by retreating into himself and avoiding emotional demands.

In other forms of day care new rules also have to be learnt, but the problems may be rather different. In a day nursery or nursery school the children will have equal rights with other children over the good things, whether they are the best tricycle or the caretaker's attention, and the main need is probably to compete successfully through assertiveness and aggression, rather than to 'appease'. Also the ambience is not domestic but play-centred; physically it will look very different from home, and there will be no one adult with whom he will be expected to form a close relationship.

There are other reasons why minded children may tend to be detached and passive, reasons which lie not so much in the child and his perception of his surroundings as in the minder and her perception of him. One of these is that minders probably reward and encourage quiet behaviour without necessarily realizing it. We have seen that their time is largely taken up with running their own large families, and they are not likely to go out of their way to bestir a quiet and apparently contented child into making demands on them. On the contrary, it seems very clear that most minders virtually equate 'quiet' with 'good', and interpret quietness as a sign that the child is settled, adapted and content, even though they half recognize that their own children were more boisterous and naughty. If the minded child makes no fuss they can get on thankfully with all their other tasks. This is different, we would suggest, from other forms of day care such as day nurseries or nursery schools where children are not likely to be rewarded by staff for sitting quietly and not doing much. There they are much more likely to be told to play and to have play activities organized for them, and there will probably also be a greater variety of things to do.

Secondly, as well as rewarding quiet behaviour, minders probably have very little tolerance of troublesome, aggressive or distressed behaviour. This may be partly because in the rush of their daily domestic round they simply have not the time to sit down with a child or hold him for however long it takes to calm, reassure and distract him. But it is not just a question of time: it must also be a great emotional strain for a minder to care for a child who clearly does not want to be there with her. Not only must she cope alone with the stress and anxiety of this, but she must also balance the minded child's needs against those of other minded children, and more especially those of her own young child. Where children continued to show disturbance or distress the minding arrangement might even be brought to an end.

The effect of this would be to increase slightly the proportion of quiet children who stay with minders and who would therefore be more likely to appear in a sample such as ours. However, disturbance was not a reason commonly given to us in explanation for arrangements having ended, so it is unlikely to be the only, or even the most important cause of the high proportion of quiet children. Again, day nurseries and nursery schools cannot get rid of disturbed or difficult children unless they are so maladjusted that they need special care, and indeed would probably see it as part of their job nowadays to care for such children.

Thirdly we wonder whether there may not be something about looking after someone else's child daily in one's own home that inhibits the formation of close emotional relationships with that child. 'Mothering' may involve a commitment to the child and his future, a commitment which is intricately bound up with a deep knowledge of the child as a unique individual. It may be difficult for a minder to make this commitment. After all, the child has his own parents to whom he returns each day after a few hours, and because she does not go into the child's home but he into hers, the minder does not get to know him in the wider context of his life. This is only speculation, but it could be one reason why some apparently warm and caring minders do not seem to have close relationships with minded children.

The question which has been lurking behind most of this discussion is whether passivity and detachment are characteristic just of minded children or of children in all forms of day care. There is very little direct evidence, but what there is suggests that children in day nurseries and nursery schools are very different.

In the study they made of day nurseries as part of the Oxford Preschool Research Project, Garland and White (1980) were interested in rather different aspects of the child's behaviour than ourselves, but their descriptions suggest that children do not generally sit around passively, and that the prevailing atmosphere is usually one of noise, bustle, activity, movement, and of aggression between children rather than passivity. The head of one of the nurseries they studied, whose particular interest was in language development, said she tried to put quieter children, and those who had been minded in particular, into a separate group for some of the time, so that they would occasionally have an opportunity to talk without being shouted down by the more assertive majority. Other indirect evidence stems from observational work on children's play done in nursery schools and playgroups by Sylva, Roy and Painter, and reported in another book in this series (1980). The children they observed spent very little time doing nothing; they also spent rather little time interacting with other children but when they did, it tended to be assertively, competitively, even aggressively. The overall impression was again not one of children who were quiet and passive, although there were some who indulged in the all-absorbing concentrated play we noticed in some of our children. Day nurseries are known usually to contain many children with difficult home backgrounds, in many cases more severe than those of our minded children. And yet one does not expect to walk into a day nursery and find anything like seven in ten children looking tired or sitting around quietly or apathetically, or not seeming to have much to do with anyone else. This is an impression, and no research has yet looked precisely at the issue, but we feel we can reasonably claim it is so. It is not that children in day nurseries and nursery schools are likely to be any better adjusted or happier than minded children, indeed there is reason to suspect that children in some day nurseries may be suffering considerably, but it looks as though detachment and passivity may be ways that children react specifically to being minded.

Myths re-assessed

What are the implications of our findings for the myths about minding that we described in our opening chapter? The first goes something like this: minding is a good form of care, and especially for babies and toddlers, because it approximates more closely than any other to being at home with mother –

which would be ideal but which unfortunately not all mothers can manage. This could be called the government sponsored myth, and is usually augmented by a reference to minding's low cost in relation to day nurseries. The second great myth, associated with the first, is that the only qualification a minder needs is to be a mother herself.

Let us consider first the idea of the minder as a mother-substitute offering the child 'close, personal continuing relationships that are so essential as the foundation of sound emotional development', even compensating him for love he may have missed out on at home, and all in an atmosphere just like home. In a very limited and rather dubious sense our results could be interpreted as supporting the claim for the homelike atmosphere: the child's day at the minder's, spent largely on the periphery of the minder's domestic routine with very little time for child-centred play, is probably similar to life at home.

That minding is emotionally the next best thing to being with mum we can see is quite untrue when we look at the large numbers of children who are passive and detached from their minders. Many of them seem rather to be biding their time until mum or dad reappear. By the same token many of the minders do not seem particularly warmly involved with the children, and the idea that they provide some kind of compensation for a lack of love from home is just wrong. Indeed the children we knew to have poor relationships with parents very often had the least warm minders, and one might even say that for these children the minder was a substitute *bad* mother, with the pattern of poor relationships between child and parent repeated between child and minder.

The second myth is that all will be well for the minded child provided the minder has had children of her own and treats him as she treats her own. This view is held by most minders and by mothers too, many of whom asked no more of a minder when they selected her than that she was a mother herself. This myth, too, is just not supported by what we found.

In fact the more one thinks about this myth the more curious, even illogical, it seems. Of course there is a practical know-how which comes of experience – how to bath a baby or put on a nappy, how to offer a potty tactfully, how much food to provide, which coughs and sneezes to take seriously, which potential hazards to be aware of in the house, and so on. Moving beyond these practicalities, however, there is no obvious reason why a minder's experience as a mother should help her in forming a different sort of relationship with someone else's child, or in recognizing his special needs and understanding his feelings. Indeed the particular predicament of the minded child, that of being separated from his mother, is specifically one in which the minder will *not* have seen her own children.

It is even possible to argue that her experience with her own children may actually be a disadvantage, in that she may have expectations about how children 'should' behave, or about the rewards she will herself derive from the relationship, which will not be met. Furthermore, if she expects minding to be just like looking after her own children, then she may interpret a child's failure to respond to her, or his persisting distress at being with her, as reflecting some inadequacy in her as a *mother*. This may be one reason why some minders find looking after such children so stressful.

The great danger of this myth is that it denies that minded children may have needs, wants, fears, and anxieties that are different from those of the minders' own children, or that their behaviour may have a different meaning. One minder complained that a minded child was very possessive about the toys he brought with him and would not share them like her own child did. In the end 'I told his mother not to let him bring toys as there was so much fighting'. In other words the minded child's possessiveness was contrasted with her own child's sharing, and not judged as expressing his insecurity or his need to possess something in a situation where another child owned everything. So it does not follow that the minder's experience with her own child will enable her to understand a child's behaviour, or his underlying feelings.

We have come to feel somewhat alarmed at the bandwagon that is running in favour of minding as the best solution for the day care needs of the working mother. In the last resort, it is probably cheapness that keeps this bandwagon rolling, rather than any deep conviction about minding's superiority over other forms of care.

What about the myths of the opposing camp? We can dismiss straight away the gross stereotype of the mercenary, uncaring woman, herding vast numbers of small children into a damp and dangerous basement with nothing to do all day. We found nothing whatever like this. But what about the claim that minders provide inferior care in unstimulating conditions, and 'do the job for their own convenience . . . because it fits with their domestic commitments, not out of informed, caring interest in children'?

We believe our results show this, too, to be largely false. It is true that minders are heavily committed domestically to their own families, who take up most of their time and who come first in their order of priorities. And it seems likely that minded children do suffer as a result. Minders are probably not providing as much attention and stimulating play as they might for children, although the toys they provide are not impoverished or inadequate by and large, nor any worse than most children would have at home. On the other hand it is emphatically not true that most minders do not have a caring interest in the children they mind. On the contrary, they are usually women who have a great affection for young children, who enjoy their company and who find meaning and satisfaction in staying at home and caring for them. If they expect a minded child to fit in with their own domestic commitments, this is no more than they expect of their own children. There are in any group always a few exceptions, but overall the minders were certainly not indifferent, or callous, or minding primarily for money; indeed one minder felt guilty about taking any money at all for looking after a child she loved dearly. It is hard to imagine a nicer or better intentioned group of minders.

A very private arrangement

Why is it, given all these good intentions, good facilities, and feelings of satisfaction and liking between minders and mothers, that no-one seemed to think there was anything wrong with so many of these detached and passive children? We have seen how some of the features implicit in the structure of minding may tend to make children quiet. We also think there are other issues fundamental to minding that make for an unquestioning acceptance all round that everything is for the best, and that most of these stem from the ambiguous and amorphous nature of what is essentially a private arrangement between two mothers.

Privacy dominates from when minder and mother first meet each other, when it does not seem very clear who has 'interviewed' whom. Who is being vetted? Who is bestowing, who receiving, the favour? And what is being judged? As we saw in Chapter 4, mothers make virtually no effort to shop around and compare minders, nor to check up on the one they are thinking of using. Similarly minders are not concerned to know anything about the children as individuals; they and the mothers seem to assume that if the hours suit the children will suit too.

We doubt that this is just a result of the widespread conviction that mothers make good minders, but believe it has much to do with the ill-defined relationship between mother and minder. Our impression is that neither knows quite how to behave: the situation is embarrassing and threatening because each is assessing the other on her qualities as a mother. How do you 'nose around' the house without giving offence? How can you risk giving offence to someone whom you want to trust with the care of your child? How do you tell the other that you disagree with her ideas of raising children? And how is one of you going, in the next few minutes, to raise the awkward subject of money? Add to this the fact that the mother, and probably the minder too, has very little experience in making business arrangements (and particularly rather awkward business arrangements possibly with friends) and that she may need to get something settled that day, and we have a recipe for quick and glazed decisions made on the basis of nothing being obviously wrong rather than on any more thorough assessment.

Awkwardness and ambiguity continue once the arrangement is under way. As we saw in Chapter 4, both minder and mother are uncertain how far they can go in influencing the care of the child while he is with the other; they both recognize the other's right to determine what goes in her own home. So the mother tends to abdicate her rights over her child while he is with the minder, even sometimes preferring not to know what goes on so that she need not do anything to change the situation. Minders and mothers are often reluctant to raise problems or to criticize each other, in part from a very natural reluctance to give offence and to tread on each other's maternal toes.

But we do not think that only reticence and delicacy are involved. There is evidence that both minders and mothers fear that their whole arrangement may collapse if they try to discuss worries over the child. Some minders feel this will just make things worse for the child who will then have to cope with being left with someone else, and the mothers clearly have a lot to lose, including their jobs, should their minders take offence and refuse to care for their children any more. So there are a number of pressures on minders and mothers to convince both themselves and each other that all is well, to avoid looking too closely, to hold their peace.

The private nature of minding makes it less accessible and accountable than other forms of day care. The minder is in her own home, in territory where she reigns supreme. However welcoming the minder may be, it is hard for the mother to feel she has a right of entry, let alone a right to discuss or question what goes on. The staff in day nurseries and nursery schools, on the other hand, although they often do regard the classroom as their territory, do not live there, and are paid employees. Parents know that they have the right to go in, even if they may feel discouraged or even intimidated.

The changing face of minding

Minders themselves have, in the last few years, erupted into widespread action, and are attempting to improve their status and standards. At local and national level they are aiming to make changes through association, debate and group pressure on local authorities. A large part of this activity seems, understandably, directed towards improving their pay and conditions. They are keen to prise money out of local social services departments for toys and equipment, and also set up centres where they can discuss things over a cup of coffee, or perhaps meet other nearby minders with whom they can form small panels to take over from each other for shopping, holidays and dental appointments.

These sorts of changes should all make life easier for minders and bring them more mutual support. More money for their efforts also seems essential: the present level of pay is absurd and exploitative for any minder wanting to put some effort into her work with minded children.

However, all this must not be confused with what will best help the *children*, which is quite a separate question. For example, setting up a toy library will not obviously benefit children whose minders already have good toys, as most of the minders in our sample had. Moreover, some of those who had not, thought that toys were unnecessary anyway, and so would be unlikely to use toy libraries. Similarly, centres for minders to meet each other during the day may well, from the *child*'s point of view, be yet one more strange and anxiety-provoking place to which his minder takes him, or yet another occasion when adults chat to each other while he lurks in the background. Of course there may be some children who adore the centre: but it is not certain that they all will. Some could feel very threatened.

One of the most doubtful innovations from the child's point of view is the system of back-up panels by which minders would cover for each other. Leaving the children at other minders' houses, for however short a time, would seem likely to alarm some of them and increase their anxiety. Emergencies are one thing, but they are very rare indeed and had virtually never arisen for our sample of minders. But agreements between minders might actually encourage them to leave the children more often when there was no emergency – for example, to pop to the shops or the hairdresser's. Covering for holidays would seem to be even worse for the children, although obviously convenient for mothers and minders. This had happened infrequently in our sample, but at least one mother felt her child had been disturbed at being left for two weeks with a stand-in minder, and had regressed over her toilet training.

It is not even clear to us that improving minders' pay will necessarily improve the lot of the *minded child*, at least in Oxfordshire. Our minders did not see minding as a job and did not really expect a living wage from it. A few were very angry at how little they got, and some would have liked more though were not really resentful. But the great majority accepted what they got in good part, and a few even felt guilty at taking what they saw as too much from mothers who could ill afford it. There was virtually no evidence that resentment over money interfered with their feelings for the children or the care they gave them. It is possible that if they were better paid, minders might feel more kindly-disposed towards some parents, which could only benefit the children, but, again, pay was not the main source of ill-feeling. Minders felt much more strongly about some mothers' cavalier and thoughtless behaviour in not keeping to arrangements.

Perhaps one way better pay for minders might benefit the children in future would be for minders who *were* prepared to make minded children the centre of their concern, and to give them more time and attention, to be paid more than other minders. This seems unlikely to happen in any systematic way as long as rates of pay continue to be haphazardly arranged in private between mother and minder, and as long as mothers continue to know so little about what happens to their child.

Meanwhile, an as yet unresolved source of embarrassment to minder and mother alike is how much minders in general should be paid. We suspect that this is an unresolvable question. What is a just return for anything so important as caring for young children? And how do you temper justice for the minder with mercy for the mother? And what standard of care should the minder be giving for the money she receives? If we consider a child being minded for 30 hours a week, the mother would have to pay £15 a week at 50p an hour, £22.50 at 75p an hour, and £30 at £1 an hour. The last is about the going rate (in 1979) for a cleaner in central Oxford, the first what most teenage baby-sitters would ask – and, incidentally, much higher than all but one of our minders were getting.

Perhaps the most important problem is that if minders ask for a reasonable payment, they may thereby price themselves out of the market and send mothers looking for cheaper, unregistered minders instead. So one possible consequence of better pay for minders is an increase in illegal minding. This would probably most affect the vulnerable children from poor or broken homes. The only way round this difficulty, as far as we can see, would be for social services departments to 'top up' minders' pay with allowances over and above what the mothers pay. That is already happening in some areas, but in the present economic climate is unlikely to be feasible on a large scale. If it is restricted to 'hardship cases' it raises the bogey of some kind of means test.

On the other hand, as we saw in Chapter 4, there were quite a few mothers who undoubtedly could have afforded to pay their minders more generously, and some were uneasy about how little they paid. One good consequence of these mothers' paying more could be that they would expect more in return. For example, they might expect the minder to set aside more time from her household chores to spend with the child. This might be one way in which the image of minding might change, although, given the minders' large families and full time-tables, it is not entirely clear how they could find more time; and there is also a danger that children whose mothers paid different rates to the same minder might be treated differently.

As well as improving minders' working conditions, some minders and social services departments have tried to improve standards of care by way of talks, lectures and group discussions. This is often referred to as 'training', but can include almost anything from the odd get-together or lecture to a series of evening classes. The content of talks and lectures is very variable, too. They may be confined to topics such as first aid, hygiene and diet, or they may include practical ways of making things with children, or even information on developmental 'milestones'.

As we saw in Chapter 1, the idea seems to be gaining acceptance in official circles that extra support and training for minders must benefit the children. Once again, though, we feel this is by no means obvious. The success of training will depend both on how many minders actually accept it, and on what it consists of. Our results would suggest problems on both counts.

In the first place the majority of minders in our survey saw no need for training for themselves. Without a major shift in attitude very few minders, and perhaps those who least need it, are likely to be involved. Secondly, those who thought some sort of course might be helpful, found some topics much more acceptable than others: popular topics nearly always had to do with health and safety, and especially with first aid. Yet it is very unlikely that first-aid lectures will do anything to improve the quality of the daily care the children receive. Accidents and serious injuries had virtually never happened to our sample. Even courses on how to make things with children would seem to offer limited scope for raising standards if the minders are too busy to put what they learn into practice.

There is a danger that the use of the word 'training' to cover an amorphous mixture of talks, discussions and so on, will give these things an aura of 'professionalism' which they do not merit and which could be very misleading. It might make everyone involved feel that minders who had taken part in them were fully equipped to mind. Yet there is no evidence so far that minders who do go to lectures and discussions are actually better minders. Many of the London minders in Mayall and Petrie's study had been on local authority training or in-service training schemes, and quite a number of our minders had had some kind of training and experience in the child care area, but neither study found it was a guarantee of better care.

It is also possible that the emphasis in training on health, first aid, play, and stimulation may distract attention from the important issue of *relationships*. Perhaps we should all be thinking much more about how to increase minders' sensitivity to children's signals, about the psychological effects of separation, about the child's perception of what is happening to him, about the signs of disturbed behaviour, and about the stress and depression to which some mothers fall prey when on their own with young children. As far as we know, these have not figured largely in the provision of 'training' so far.

Can anything be done?

If there are some intrinsic features of minding that work against the children's well-being, does that mean that nothing can be done to improve it? We must say at the outset that we do not feel that the picture is very optimistic, for two reasons.

In the first place it seems likely that even in areas with high nursery provision, children will continue to be sent to minders from families with problems of one kind or another, since those mothers are likely to be the ones most impelled to work. Indeed, some social services departments are turning more frequently to minders for care of 'priority' children. In so far as children with home difficulties seem to be more vulnerable and to do less well with a minder, we can expect to continue to find quiet and detached minded children.

Secondly, people are not likely to change their practices unless they are convinced that it is necessary, so before anything else can change, we believe that the whole image of minding as an extension of motherhood will have to go. This image is reflected not just in the knowledge thought to be required but in the regimen, too. The minders saw no reason to abandon their household tasks for the minded children, any more than they did for their own children, and they resisted any idea that they should become anything resembling a playgroup. At the same time the mothers and minders of the older children clearly thought that something more than domesticity was needed, and most of the three- and four-year-olds were sent to playgroups as well. That did not always seem to be a very fruitful combination, however, since some of these children were among the quietest and most detached of all. We do not know, unfortunately, how they behaved at the playgroup.

We can assume that the conviction will be hard to change. Not only do the actors on stage – the minders, mothers and social services departments – have it written into their scripts, but their prompters off-stage, the DHSS, see to it that they do not forget their lines.

Because of the problems embedded in the structure of minding as practised at present, we cannot join wholeheartedly in the present drive for its piecemeal modification and expansion, particularly since we fear that the sorts of measures being proposed are not likely to help the children. On the other hand we must accept that, for the moment, minding is here to stay and may very well increase in the short run, as the recessionary axe continues to fall on nursery provision. So we must somehow find ways of improving minding and of avoiding some of the pitfalls.

For the rest of this chapter we shall consider how this might be done. We do not intend to set out a blueprint for a new minding service. That would be presumptuous on the basis of one small study. Instead we shall try to use our results to point to where improvement or further investigation seem necessary, and make some suggestions.

First, we can say that there are many vital questions still unanswered. Research reports often conclude by calling for yet more research! This book is no exception. Before we can say anything very definitive about minding we need more answers. For example, there is much we do not know about the comparative effects of different sorts of day care. Our study was not comparative, so we cannot be sure whether or how far the quiet children would have been just the same had they been in some other form of care such as a day nursery, a crèche, or an all-day playgroup. Do some forms of care suit particular children, or are there some blessed individuals who will thrive anywhere and others who will always suffer?

We do know that we are not alone in finding minded children quiet. Mayall and Petrie found the same among London minded children. More recently a specialist worker in another London borough wrote, anecdotally, of minded children becoming 'unnaturally good' once they have settled; she described how, in the groups she ran for minders 'the [minded] children go straight off and play, often with great pleasure and concentration, and hardly bother the adults at all' (Corbishley, 1979). In their current work Mayall and Petrie have made a start on a comparative study which looks at children in day nurseries and with minders, and we need more research along these lines.

We also know very little about the everyday lives of children at home with their mothers, what sorts of behaviour are considered normal or abnormal, and whether notions about this differ across social classes. Some recent work on this, as yet unpublished, has been carried out by Corinne Hutt and her colleagues at Keele University and by Judy Dunn in Cambridge, both using combined observations and interviews. These should provide a background against which to think about children being cared for outside the home. In other words, how does home life compare with different forms of day care?

One particular aspect of development about which we need to know more is language acquisition in minded children. Mayall and Petrie found that many of their London minded children were below the level of speech normal for their age and, although we did not use a systematic language test, we too found evidence that a minority were backward in speech or had other language difficulties. We do not have any evidence that being minded actually causes language retardation, and it could be that children who are slow to develop speech anyway are more likely to end up being minded. On the other hand it does seem likely that the detached and passive children who interacted very little with their minders were losing the opportunity to practise and develop their speech.

There has been much discussion about the sorts of environment that best foster the acquisition of language, but few studies have compared speech of the same children in different settings. However, a very interesting study by Barbara Tizard has recently done this, by looking at children talking with their mothers and with their nursery school teachers (1979). She found that, irrespective of social class, conversations between children and mothers were more complex, had more exchanges, and elicited more from the children than ones between children and teachers. She explains this partly by the teacher's having to give attention to many children, but she also suggests that it is due in part to the teacher's lack of knowledge about the child and his home, about his past and his future. We have already touched on a similar point about minders: that however fond a minder is of children, she may not see the minded child as someone for whom she has a lasting commitment and responsibility, and about whom she therefore needs to know a great deal. Clearly we need to know more about children's conversations with minders, and how they compare with those with mothers and other caretakers.

We also need a clearer understanding of the significance of the quiet and detached behaviour we observe in many children. Is it really a rating of unhappiness? Is their development generally, as well as their language, being adversely affected by this lack of involvement with adults? Certainly some of the quiet children seemed to be having difficulty relating to other children, although not all by any means of them. And does this behaviour persist? At the moment we just do not have enough evidence to answer many of these questions. Some is emerging from a longitudinal study by Naomi Richman and her colleagues at the Institute of Child Health in London: they have found that behaviour problems in preschool children do seem to persist into school and are associated with learning difficulties there.

This brings us on to yet another question. How do children cope with the transition to primary school? What difference does it make whether they have previously stayed at home with mum or have been in some kind of day care? Again, we know of one project under way at the National Foundation for Educational Research which is following groups of children with different kinds of preschool experience, among them minded children, and their results should help us to see how minded children compare with others.

Research of this sort takes time and money. In the meantime there are a number of practical changes based on some of our findings and interpretations that would clearly be worth trying out – even though we have not always conclusively proved that they will help. They concern both mothers and minders equally, but it is probably easier for minders to take the initiative in introducing them since they are in a better position to organize themselves.

1. First, common sense demands a change in the way children start at minders'. Greater care should be taken to help each child to get to know his minder, and to settle him in when he starts. More information should be exchanged about him as a person, about his likes and ways and special words for things, his home circumstances, his previous experience of care, his worries, and so on. We believe it would help if minders had clear rules about this and refused to take children they had not met more than once. Perhaps they could talk to mothers about this when first approached; or perhaps if mothers contacted social services for names of registered minders, the specialist workers could discuss it with them. However the change is managed, the present system whereby some minders and mothers treat children with about as little consideration as parcels left *poste restante* must go.

2. We suggest that the minder should pay at least one visit to the child's home early on. This would give her the opportunity to see how he normally behaves at home, and she would also learn something about his home life which would help to provide continuity for him in their conversations at her house.

3. Ways must also be found for the mother and minder to overcome their defensiveness and talk to each other about the child and his progress. Perhaps the minder could help in this by making it clear at the outset that she wants the mother to know all about what happens to her child. She could encourage her to come in and see, and to join in. This would grow easier anyway if it became customary for mothers to stay at the minders over several days at the start of the arrangement. Perhaps minders could make it a condition that on one day a week they sit down together and talk about the child, and especially compare notes on how he behaves with each of them.

4. It might help the minded child if he were positively encouraged to bring some of his own toys to the minder's, and if he were given a corner, drawer, or shelf that was clearly his – perhaps with his name on it. The minder would have to accept that he might refuse to share these toys, at least to start with, and might want to defend them staunchly from seizure by other children. She should support him in this rather than admonish him. There might be other ways of helping him to feel in control, such as putting some of his pictures up on her wall rather than always sending him home with them.

5. Minders should be on the watch for quiet children who seem very good and well-behaved, and who do not make demands; also for children who sit passively not doing very much, and those who play in a very concentrated way at single activities for long periods.

6. Minders should spend less time on their household chores when minded children are there, and try to centre the day more than at present around doing things with them and talking to them. We are not suggesting, though, that they

should never do domestic chores; obviously children enjoy and learn from 'helping' around the houses, and shared household activities can be opportunities for conversation.

7. Mothers and minders should be alert to the problems of older children, those starting at the minder's when they are already over three years old. Minders may have to be extra patient in winning these children's confidence, prepared to devote considerable time to them, and not put off by their initial indifference and lack of responsiveness.

How can these suggestions be made acceptable to the majority of mothers and minders when some of them clearly contradict the prevailing convictions about minding? It is indeed difficult to answer this, but we see hope in the undoubted good will of many minders and their current concern to organize and improve. Perhaps some of their energy could be channelled into these rather different sorts of innovations.

We should like to see social services departments and minders working together towards improvement. In Oxfordshire the Social Services Department has already produced a pamphlet for the guidance of minders. We would propose a different or additional booklet which spelled out the sorts of difficulties that might be encountered, and the sort of behaviour to be expected from minded children and what it might mean. This booklet should also offer advice on how to set up arrangements with mothers that would take into account the particular needs and characteristics of individual children and leave open paths of communication between mothers and minders.

We should particularly like to see such a guidance booklet written *jointly* for minders and mothers. We believe there is a danger that minders, in their search for status and recognition as part of a day-care service, may become somewhat exclusive. Their national association, while accepting parents as members, is mainly geared to minders. And we have seen that many minders regard themselves as in some way morally superior to the mothers whose children they mind. Yet, even as minders ask to be seen as 'part of the pattern of child care (i.e. as a social worker rather than something to be solved by a social worker)' so we would urge that they and the social services departments stop considering working mothers of young children as problems, and accept them as partners and colleagues – indeed, experts about their own children – rather than as adversaries in a conflict where the losers will always be the children.

We suggest a booklet partly because, when we were working with groups of minders watching the BBC television series *Other People's Children*, many said they found the accompanying booklet interesting and helpful. Indeed they were much more enthusiastic about it than about the programmes themselves. However we should also like to see small gatherings of minders organized to discuss the sorts of problems which arise and the sorts of changes we are proposing. Small groups of this kind, under experienced leaders, might be more fruitful in changing attitudes than lectures which are more remote and didactic. We should like to see mothers included in equal numbers in these groups also.

These groups might be used as well to teach minders (and mothers) to observe the behaviour of minded children. The observational techniques devised by Kathy Sylva and our other colleagues in the Preschool Research Group might be used in this way. They have already been taken up nationally by the PPA for use in training playgroup leaders, and a manual written by Avril Holmes and Linnet McMahon (1979) has been published by them. David Wood and others of our colleagues have developed techniques for teachers and play-group leaders to use in looking at their own interaction with children. These, too, are being further refined and adapted by Linnet McMahon and Yvonne Cranstoun for use in training. They could well be useful in helping minders to increase their awareness of their behaviour with minded children.

As well as direct efforts to get minders and mothers thinking and to change their attitudes, it might be possible to bring about changes by making registration a more selective process. However it is very difficult to see how it can ever be more than a minimum safeguard, unless some more precise criteria than we could identify for assessing good minders can be found. On the other hand specialist workers could perhaps make more use of dissuasion, by emphasising to prospective minders the problems and hazards of minding: that they cannot just expect to fit it in around their other domestic chores, that it is very much more complex than just tucking another small child under your maternal wing – and may sometimes be very distressing. They could also, perhaps, produce some kind of code of practice which might require minders, as a condition of registration, to take part in group discussions and other teaching techniques over a period of time.

There were some minders in our sample whom we felt should not have been registered, and specialist workers could find out more about prospective minders and be firmer in discouraging unsuitable ones. Some of those we interviewed had, for example, turned to minding because they were depressed or anxious; others had quite severe and demoralizing family troubles including physical or mental problems in their own children; others seemed to be socially isolated women who described themselves as not wanting to mix with others and preferring to keep themselves to themselves; and a few seemed to be rather obsessional, over-tidy people. Although taking in a minded child may be a welcome relief and distraction from private troubles, it must be wrong to use minded children in this way. It may be that some of these troubles were not evident when the specialist worker visited, but it does not take a great deal of effort to find out about them.

We are aware that some social services departments take the view that it is better to register doubtful applicants and keep an eye on them, on the grounds that they will otherwise mind illegally. We would query the sense of this. We found that in Oxfordshire, at least, minders were rarely visited, and the Social Services Department did not know which minders were currently minding children, let alone manage to influence their standards. Yet mothers do attach some meaning to registration as an under-writing of standards, so it is important that it should actually be that.

This raises the question of whether minding would be improved if minders were visited more frequently. We think that would depend on what the visits involved. We had the impression that the minders who were visited saw the call as primarily intended to help *them*, as a friendly check that they had no problems with the minded child. Yet, as we saw, they almost invariably described the children as 'no trouble'. Increasing the frequency of this sort of visiting would not, we think, do much to improve life for minded children generally, although there were rare cases where the visitor would have seen obviously unsatisfactory conditions.

For visiting to be effective it should focus more on the *child*; there should be much greater emphasis on observing the child and his behaviour directly – watching in particular for quiet, passive, undemanding or detached behaviour. The specialist worker should also visit the child in his own home so that his behaviour in the two situations can be assessed, and also so that she can discover whether there are any home difficulties which might be affecting him. Some further procedures would have to be tried out if she felt the child was not thriving. Perhaps she could bring the mother and minder together, or get them both to come to one of the group meetings to discuss the child. There is a need to explore how this could best be done.

Social services departments might also try to keep up-to-date records not just of which minders are registered in their areas but also of which children are being minded and why they leave their minders. Such records would reveal the children who are moved around a great deal (which might be a sign that they are disturbed or distressed) and the minders who seem unable to keep arrangements going. These minders, children and, indeed, mothers, might need closer attention than the others.

This brings us finally to the question of children in special need, the 'priority' children whom social services themselves place with minders and for whom they pay. By definition these children are likely to come from homes suffering from tension or stress; they may even be contributing to the stress for the mother, for example, if they are hyperactive or difficult to control. It is just these children who are most likely to be quiet, detached or passive at the minder's. They are also more likely to be overtly disturbed, even withdrawn, and to have language difficulties. Clearly, minding is no easy or obvious solution for these children and minders may have considerable difficulty in coping with them, so that more active intervention by specialist workers may be needed. Indeed, everything we have proposed to help minded children generally applies with even greater emphasis to the priority children.

Our proposals would be bound to cost a good deal of money. Persuading people to give up deeply entrenched views cannot be achieved through a lecture here, a group discussion there, as Brian Jackson has claimed. Rather it involves a considerable investment of time and specialist work in the way of organizing, supervising, monitoring and supporting minders, mothers and children over long periods. We hope that as a result of this study and the earlier one by Mayall and Petrie, the DHSS will give up its comforting but ill-founded belief that the minder is a substitute mother, and stop drifting down the road of the cheap, easy option.

Once they do, and more money is made available for minding, other forms of day care become *comparatively* less expensive. This in turn means that it becomes possible to diversify, to develop a whole range of care for children, such as day nurseries, crèches, all-day playgroups, home play-groups, children's centres and nursery schools – perhaps even tax relief on wages paid to those coming into homes to look after the children, or, for mothers who do not want to work, pay to stay at home with their own children. Given the doubts that these studies have raised about minding it seems vital that options should be kept open and alternatives encouraged, at least until we know more about the advantages and disadvantages of different forms of care and about which will most help different children to thrive.

This study has been about minding in one county, Oxfordshire. We do not know how far Oxfordshire represents the rest of the country, but it is probably not untypical of other largely rural and small town areas, although it is obviously not at all typical of large conurbations, inner city boroughs, or declining industrial regions with their concentrations of poverty and deprivation. It is true that Oxfordshire has very few day nurseries, so it may have more minded children with home difficulties than would be found, say, in an inner city area where such children would qualify for day nursery places. On the other hand it may have less need for day nurseries. It is not a deprived county, and has good housing and very few single-parent families – to look only at two common measures of deprivation. Such social problems as it has pale into insignificance compared with those of our inner cities.

Minding in Oxfordshire probably compares favourably with minding in many areas. The fact that we found so few children at each minder's, compared with the London study, and found so many minders who could not find children to mind, supports this. But it brings little comfort to know that perhaps even more minded children in other areas are not thriving.

Nor, we realize, can the tenor of this book be of comfort to minders or to mothers of minded children. What minder or mother wants to know that in spite of the minder's good will and experience, the child she is caring for may not be happy even though he does not fuss? Or that his failure to thrive may be attributable in part to minding as a form of care? Yet we hope that minders will see that we recognize the good will and valuable qualities that many of them have, and understand that this book is not just more bad press. Similarly, we hope the mothers will not feel that we are yet one more admonitory finger wagging in their direction because they choose to work rather than stay at home with their children. As we have said, there are no villains nor heroines in our story.

Yet there are victims. These children cannot speak for themselves, and it is for us, all of us, to speak for them, and to demand from policy makers more generosity and concern and a greater commitment to improving standards than they have so far shown.

Short bibliography

ASSOCIATION OF COUNTY COUNCILS and ASSOCIATION OF METROPOLITAN AUTHORITIES (1977) *Under Fives: a Local Authority Associations Study.* London: ACC/AMA.

BONE, M. (1977) *Preschool Children and the Need for Daycare.* OPCS Survey No. 1031. London: HMSO.

BRITISH ASSOCIATION OF SOCIAL WORKERS (1978) *Children Under Five.* London: BASW.

BROWN, G. W. and HARRIS, T. O. (1978) *Social Origins of Depression.* London: Tavistock; New York: Free Press.

BURCHALL, A. (1978) In *Who Minds?* February newsletter of the National Childminding Association.

CALDWELL, B. (1967) Descriptive evaluations of child development and of developmental settings. *Pediatrics*, **40**, 46–54.

CENTRAL POLICY REVIEW STAFF (1978) *Services for Young Children of Working Mothers.* London: HMSO.

COLEMAN, J., WOLKIND, S. and ASHLEY, L. (1977) Symptoms of behaviour disturbance and adjustment to school. *Journal of Child Psychology and Psychiatry*, **18**, 201–9.

COMMUNITY RELATIONS COMMISSION (1975) *Who Minds?* London: CRC.

CORBISHLEY, H. (1979) *Contact.* February, 10–12.

CORNWALL SOCIAL SERVICES DEPARTMENT (1974) A look at childminding. Research and development study No. 9.

DEPARTMENT OF EDUCATION AND SCIENCE and DEPARTMENT OF HEALTH AND SOCIAL SECURITY (1976) Low cost provision for the under-fives. Papers from a conference held at the Civil Service College, Sunningdale.

DEPARTMENT OF EDUCATION AND SCIENCE and DEPARTMENT OF HEALTH AND SOCIAL SECURITY (1978) Coordination of services for children under five. LA Social Services Letter LASSL (78)1, HN (78)5, S47/24/013.

DOUGLAS, J. (1975) Early hospital admissions and later disturbance of behaviour and learning. *Developmental Medicine and Child Neurology*, **17**, 456.

DOUGLAS, J., LAWSON, A., COOPER, J. and COOPER, E. (1968) Family interaction and the activities of young children. *Journal of Child Psychology and Psychiatry*, **9**, 157–71.

EQUAL OPPORTUNITIES COMMISSION (1978) *I Want to Work but What About the Kids?* London: EOC.

GARLAND, C. and WHITE, S. (1980) *Children and Day Nurseries.* London: Grant McIntyre; Ypsilanti, Michigan: High/Scope.

HARROW BRANCH OF THE NATIONAL CAMPAIGN FOR NURSERY EDUCATION and HARROW SOCIAL SERVICES DEPARTMENT (1975) The demand for preschool provision.

HEINICKE, C. M. and WESTHEIMER, I. J. (1975) *Brief Separations.* London: Longman.

IMBER, V. (1977) *A Classification of the English Personal Social Services Authorities. DHSS Statistical and Research Series No. 16.* London: HMSO.

JACKSON, B. (1973) The childminders. *New Society*, **26**, 521. 29 November.

JACKSON, B. (1976) Paper given at the conference on low cost provision for the under fives held at the Civil Service College, Sunningdale.

JULIAN, R. (1977) *Brought to Mind*. New Zealand Council for Educational Research.

KING, R., RAYNES, N. and TIZARD, J. (1971) *Patterns of Residential Care*. London and Boston: Routledge & Kegan Paul.

LAWSON, A. and INGLEBY, J. D. (1974) Daily routines of preschool children: effects of age, birth order, sex, and social class, and developmental correlates. *Psychological Medicine*, **4**, 399–415.

LEACH, P. (1979) *Who Cares?* Harmondsworth and New York: Penguin.

LONDON COUNCIL OF SOCIAL SERVICES (1977) *Childminding in London*. London: LCSS.

MAYALL, B. and PETRIE, P. (1977) *Minder, Mother and Child*. London: University of London Institute of Education.

NEWTON, D., HARRIS, M. and BRYANT, B. (1978) *Television and Childminders*. London: SSRC.

McMAHON, L. and HOLMES, A. (1979) *Learning from Observing*. London: Pre-school Playgroups Association.

OSBORNE, B. (1975) Working mothers and childminding in the central district of Lewisham. Lewisham Council for Community Relations unpublished report.

PETERS, D. L. (1972) Day care homes: a Pennsylvania profile. Philadelphia: Center for Human Sciences Development, College of Human Development, Pennsylvania State University.

PHILLIPS, M. (1976) Who's minding the children? *New Society*, **38**, 310.

PINES, M. (1966) Day care: the problem nobody wants to face. In Pines, M. *Revolution in Learning*. New York and London: Harper & Row.

PLOWDEN, LADY (1976) Paper given at the conference on low cost provision for the under fives held at the Civil Service College, Sunningdale.

QUINTON, D. and RUTTER, M. (1976) Early hospital admissions and later disturbances of behaviour. *Developmental Medicine and Child Neurology*, **18**, 4, 447–59.

RICHMAN, N., STEVENSON, J. E. and GRAHAM, P. J. (1975) Prevalence of behaviour problems in three-year-old children: an epidemiological study in a London borough. *Journal of Child Psychology and Psychiatry*, **16**, 277–87.

RUTTER, M. (1971) Parent-child separation: psychological effects on the children. *Journal of Child Psychology and Psychiatry*, **12**, 233–60.

RUTTER, M. (1972) *Maternal Deprivation Reassessed*. Harmondsworth and New York: Penguin.

RUTTER, M. and BROWN, G. W. (1966) The reliability and validity of measures of family life and relationships in families containing a psychiatric patient. *Social Psychiatry*, **1**, 38–50.

SCHAFFER, R. (1977) *Mothering*. London: Open Books/Fontana; Cambridge, Massachusetts: Harvard University Press.

SHINMAN, S. M. (1979) Focus on childminders. Inner London Pre-school Playgroups Association.

SMITH, T. and HARRIS, M. (1978) A preschool primer. *The Times Educational Supplement*, 21 July.

SYLVA, K. D., ROY, C. and PAINTER, M. (1980) *Childwatching at Playgroup and Nursery School*. London: Grant McIntyre; Ypsilanti, Michigan: High/Scope.

THAYER, P. (1976) Where can he best be cared for: childminder, day nursery or day care centre? Paper given at a conference at the Royal Society of Health.

TIZARD, B. (1979) Language at home and at school. In Cazden, C. B. and Harvey, D. (eds) *Language in Early Childhood Education*. Washington, DC: National Association for the Education of Young Children.

TIZARD, J., MOSS, P. and PERRY, J. (1976) *All Our Children*. London: Temple Smith/New Society.

TIZARD, J. (1976) Paper given at the conference on low cost provision for the under fives held at the Civil Service College, Sunningdale.

TRADES UNION CONGRESS (1977) *The Under Fives*. London: TUC.

WAGNER, M. and WAGNER, M. (1976) *The Danish National Childcare System*. Boulder, Colorado: Westview Press.

WILLMOTT, P. and CHALLIS, L. (1977) *The Groveway Project: an Experiment in Salaried Childminding*. London: Department of the Environment.

Index

single parent families, see lone
   parent families
sleeping
   at minders', 80
   at home, 80–81, 123–4
social security, 57
Social Services Departments, 1, 3,
   5, 9, 10, 16, 224, 226, 231–4
   Oxfordshire, 38, 124
      contact with minders, 30–32,
      102–5, 198, 233–4
      list of registered minders, 68,
      70, 233
      minders' satisfaction with, 104
      organization of minding, 30–32,
      223, 231
      payment for priority children,
      103, 210
social workers
   Oxfordshire, 30, 102–5, 124
specialist childminding workers,
   227, 233
   Oxfordshire, 30–31, 32, 102–5,
   124
speech development, 16, 228

Sunningdale conference, 12, 13, 17
support services for minders, 9–16,
   29–31, 221–5, 231–5

toilet training, 82, 192, 222
toy libraries, 11, 31, 221
toys, 42, 104
   at minders', 41, 149–51, 163, 190,
   204, 208, 212
   at home, 41, 150–51
training of minders, 3, 9, 11, 13, 14,
   16, 30, 31, 50–51, 116, 190,
   224–5

unregistered minders, 32, 33, 34,
   223
   satisfaction with, 6
   numbers, 2, 4, 6, 7, 25, 34

weighting of data, 36–7
working mothers, 2, 3, 8, 14, 15, 21,
   25, 26, 28, 33, 44, 64, 107,
   118–40, 202–3, 218, 225, 232,
   236